Sidonia's Seam Binding

Sidonia's Seam Binding

A Holocaust Dressmaker's Daughter Discovers Her Style

Hanna Perlstein Marcus

© 2023 by Hanna Perlstein Marcus. All rights reserved. No part of this memoir may be excerpted, reproduced, copied, or duplicated by any method whatsoever unless specifically approved by the author. This prohibition includes, but is not limited to recording, taping, and entering text into electronic storage and retrieval systems.

Published by Buttonhole Publishing, Vernon, Connecticut

Designed by Acorn Studio

Most of the characters in this memoir have fictitious names but are based on real people. In some cases, the author has used characters' real names, particularly when referring to her relatives.

The real events described in these pages are largely founded on actual occurrences. The remembrances stem solely from the author's memory of events or her mother's stories and include neither interviews with nor the perspective of any other person.

ISBN: 978-0-9979712-2-4 (paperback)
ISBN: 978-0-9979712-3-1 (ebook)

*To my mother,
Sidonia Perlstein,
an extraordinary
maven of style*

Her children rise up, and call her blessed...

—*The Book of Proverbs, 31:28*

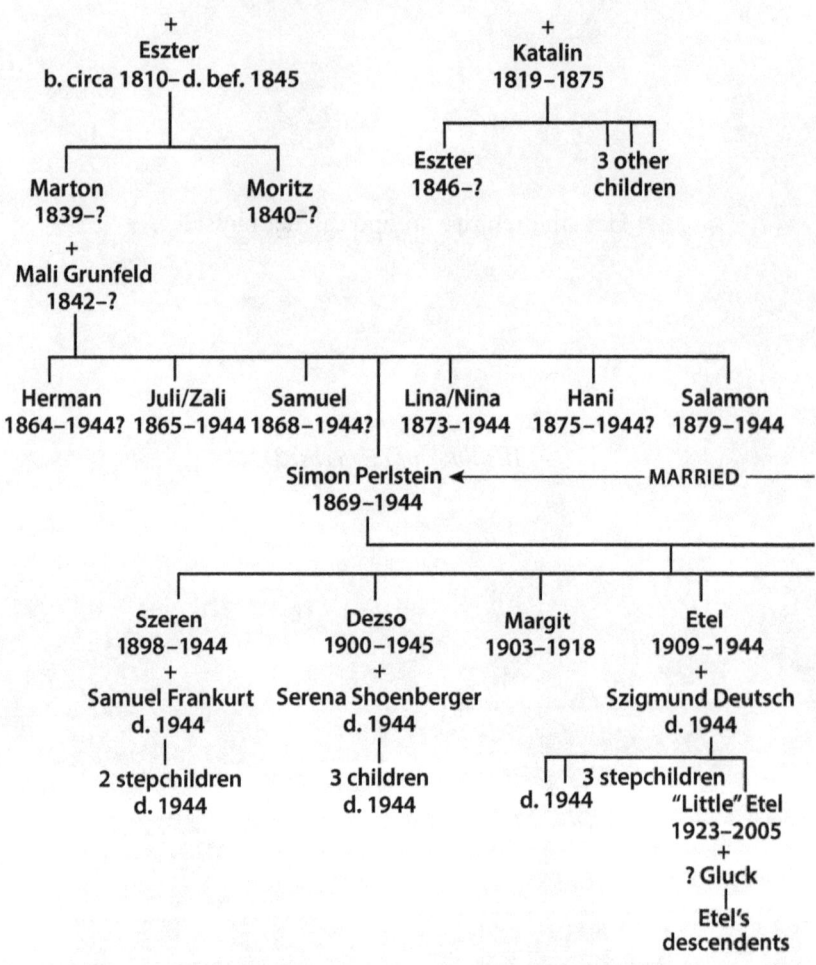

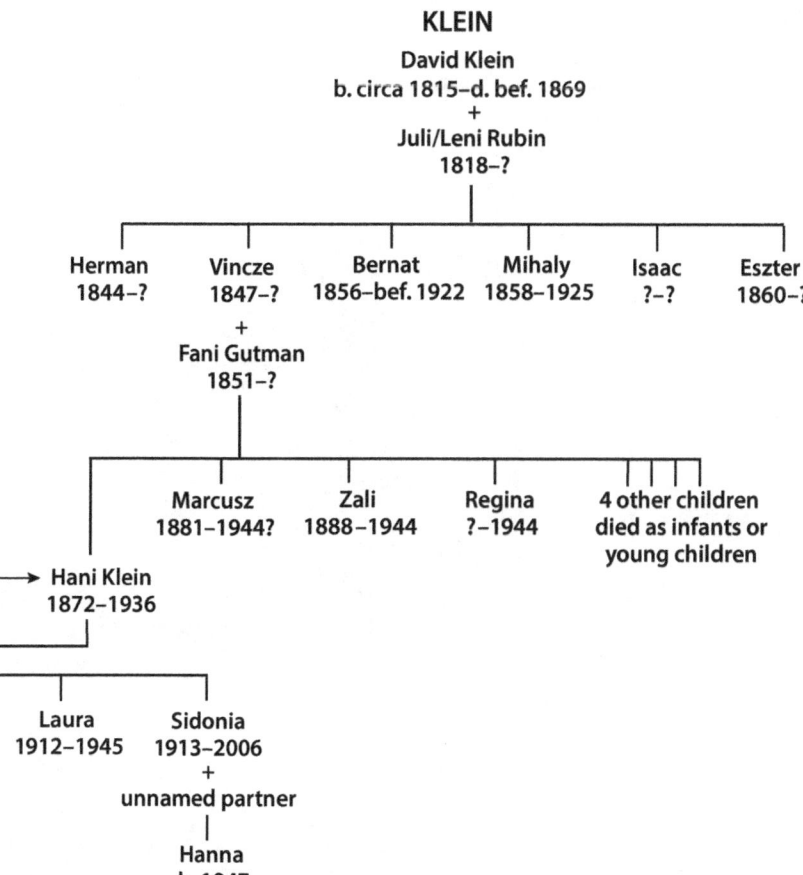

Contents

Author's Note to Readers xiii
Preface xv
Prologue xix

1 Pattern Alterations 21
2 The New Fabrics 25
3 Basting 29
4 Hand-Sewing 35
5 Bonded Fabrics 39
6 Darts 43
7 Train Yourself 51
8 Grain in Fabric 57
9 Preparation of Fabric for Cutting 61
10 Patterns 69
11 Bias Binding 75
12 Hidden Button Loop 81
13 Fabric Belt Loops 91
14 Directional Stitching 103
15 Pressure on Presser Foot 107
16 Fitting a Garment 113
17 Assembling a Garment 123

18	Simulated Kick Pleat	129
19	Facings	133
20	Plackets	139
21	Tailor's Tacks	151
22	Yardstick	163
23	Tension of Thread	175
24	Buttons	179
25	Check-List for Trouble Spots	185
26	Zippers	195
27	One-Way Design	199
28	Gussets	203
29	Self-Fringe	209
30	Marking the Hemline	217
31	Fabric Finishes	227
32	Gathers	233
33	Tape Measure and Style	237
34	Thread and Needle	243

Acknowledgments	247
Bibliography	251
Illustration Credits	257

Author's Note to Readers

In the *Sidonia's Thread* books, I have opened up my heart, memory, and imagination to you, the reader. In this volume, I have also done something more: I have shared an imagined course of my mother's life as though I did not exist. Essentially, this is my attempt to gain additional insight into my mother's character and behavior beyond what arose from my observations of her actual life, which I have concurrently recounted. I hope this alternative reality will enhance your understanding of her, as well.

I have used italics when referring to foreign words or to pieces of correspondence, either in letter or note form. Most of the italics in this book are in sections where I have imagined the events (although the surrounding details and settings in which they occurred may be real) to distinguish those events from real happenings. Occasionally, italics indicate my inner thoughts.

Research from books and articles shed further light on the attitudes, behaviors, events, genealogy, history, social work practice, and settings mentioned in this book. Listings of those references may be found in the Bibliography. In addition, a listing of the credits for all photographs, documents, and illustrations used in the book are detailed in the Illustration Credits.

Finally, all chapter titles and chapter epigraphs have been excerpted from *Coats & Clark's Sewing Book: Newest Methods from A to Z*, Educational Bureau, Coats & Clark, Inc., New York, 1967. They have been reproduced with the permission of Coats & Clark, Inc. A more complete listing of this reference may also be found in the Bibliography.

Preface

"You writing da book now, Hani, right? You know, da book about my life? I tink it make a very good story, Han."

My mother always wanted me to write a book about certain events in her life, particularly her home life in Hungary and some of her Holocaust experiences. Since the exact topics to be covered always remained vague and undefined, I was not sure whether she wanted me to write her biography, a work of fiction based on true events, or an account based on a series of interviews with her to take place at some unidentified time in the future.

> Inevitably, I would reply, "Well, Ma, I'm pretty busy these days, you know. At some point, we'll have to sit down and talk about what you would like me to write. But right now, I just don't have time to write a book."
>
> "Don't forget about it," she warned. "You da only von who can do it."
>
> "I know, Ma. I definitely won't forget. Don't worry."

I was flattered that she had enough faith in my writing skills to entrust me with penning any story about her life. While it was true that I was consistently busy, the reason I postponed any thought of a literary project based on my mother's life was more fundamental: I did not know what to say.

If a book were to be an account of my mother's life experiences, it would have to leave out all the parts that she was never able to divulge. There was no reason to believe that she would have revealed them just because she was ready to put her story to print. At best, I thought it would have been an account of selected, scattered events that occurred in the life of a courageous single Hungarian woman who had tragically lost her entire family, survived the brutality of the Holocaust, and became a noted designer and dressmaker in America. As fragmented as it may have been, it probably would still have made an admirable and moving story.

By necessity, that tale would have left out salient pieces of her life, such as the series of events at the displaced persons camp after the war, when she mysteriously produced a child out of wedlock. That set of events sharply changed the trajectory of her life even further, leading both to her reclusive, lonely existence, and to her driving ambition to develop her design and dressmaking genius.

Lacking a fuller picture of her life, including these missing pieces, I was not comfortable writing about it, so I postponed the task at every opportunity. I postponed it for so long that it was not until my mother's passing that I finally felt ready to write. The year of her death also marked the beginning of my contemplation of how I could write the book she so desired.

Then it came to me: the story would be about my life's journey with my mother in America. How did a mother and daughter alone in the world manage to lead productive and fulfilling lives in the land they adopted after the ashes of the Holocaust? It would include my own observations of our visit to the land of my ancestors. This trip instilled in me a powerful urge to tell the story about how the Perlstein family's remnant—my mother—had made her family proud, while also exploring my own place within this family.

In writing the first story, I took on the role of narrator, recounting some pivotal events in our lives together. I knew, in the process, my mother would become the focus for the reader. How could she not? Combined with illustrations and correspondence I uncovered by chance in her nightstand drawer and the sewing methods described in her only sewing tutorial, I had enough to build a compelling tale. Although I understood that she would have resented the revelations in my writing, at least for a while, I could now divulge events in my mother's life that she would never have revealed herself. They would fill in the missing pieces to the story she envisioned. Several years later, *Sidonia's Thread* came to fruition.

As I spoke about my story at libraries, universities, community centers, religious organizations, and conferences, I learned that readers wanted to know more about my mother, and although lesser so, about me. My early childhood among the greenhorns in my survivor community, and the variety of characters and events of my upbringing, were of particular interest. My readers' curiosity inspired me to write a second volume, *Surviving Remnant*, which focused on my childhood.

Yet, I found I still had more to say. I had not written about the alternative reality of my mother's life that I had spun in my thoughts over many years. Based solely in my imagination, it had become a companion story that my mind visited from time to time, side by side with the one we had truly lived together—a tale of my mother's life as though I had never been born. Through the years, I had found solace, and perhaps an absolving of guilt, in devising an account of a different life experience for her, which was dominated by happiness and joy, but also included some disappointment and loss.

With the help again of the methods described in my mother's only sewing book, I decided to include this alternative reality in a new volume, along with my assessment of how my life turned out as a result of my mother's influence. Combined with deepened perspectives and supplements to some stories recounted in the previous two volumes, this last book in the *Sidonia's Thread* trilogy, *Sidonia's Seam Binding*, enhances Sidonia's and my stories, while it adds to my own understanding of my elusive mother.

Prologue

> Suitable for all fabrics, especially for fabrics that ravel easily ... Topstitch binding to right side of hem ¼" from cut edge, as shown, easing it to fabric. Overlap end, turned under as shown. Place work on ironing board, wrong side out. — "Hems," page 102

She finished every hem with lace seam binding. No hemstitches were ever exposed. She did this not only to ensure that no raveling of the fabric threads would occur, but also to add beauty to the garment's bottom inside edge. The pleasing veneer of the seam binding mirrored her own pattern of covering up her true feelings of sadness, shame, and resentment with outward pride, pseudo-confidence, and pleasant conversation.

CHAPTER 1

Pattern Alterations

> The principle of good pattern alteration is to change the measurements indicated without changing the pattern's essential outline ... through body of pattern, by folding to reduce size or cutting and spreading to increase. This method preserves the shape of the outer pattern. — "Patterns," page 135

I have been a loner my whole life. I follow in my mother's footsteps.

My feelings of aloneness really hit home on the day I turned twelve, as we moved to a new neighborhood in Springfield. It was August 29, 1959, and my legs felt unusually heavy and stiff as I faced the steep flight of stairs leading up to our new rented living quarters, a second-floor unit in a 1920s-era two-family house on Maryland Street. My homemade pink cotton camisole and shorts set stuck to my body like a wet sponge in the scorching heat of the afternoon.

> "Oy, Hanele, ve gotta get our tings up da stairs. You can't stop just like dat, you know," my mother said, as she gently prodded me to lift my legs and start bringing our belongings inside.
>
> "I know, Ma. Just trying to get used to this new place. I hope we're doing the right thing, moving to another part of town."

The Forest Park area was an improvement over our previous small apartment on Osgood Street in the North End. Although I had sometimes imagined this move, I knew it would take us away from the only part of the city I knew. More importantly, we would be separated from our close-knit refugee community, known in Yiddish as *di grine* [pronounced "di-green-eh"] or in English as "the greenhorns." Who would be there now if I ever fell down these steep stairs or if my mother and I needed to be consoled if something went wrong, like a downturn in our finances? Although I understood, realistically, they had all moved away from our old home anyway, my resistance to change took over. I was not sure it was such a good move after all.

Di grine at the beach, around 1953. The author is the child in the first row, far right. Sidonia is in the back row, second from the right.

"Dat's okay. You gonna be alright. It's vhat I been doing my whole life. Just trying to get used to anoder place. You be fine in a little vhile," she responded, shrugging her shoulders. "Tzi nisht azoy geferlekh," she added in Yiddish. Of course, she would think it was not so terrible.

"An don't forget, it's your birsday an dat make it really special," she reminded me.

"It does make it special, I guess," I said, my dour voice revealing my true feelings.

My mother was right when she told me that she had spent her whole life trying to get used to another place. Well, not really her whole life, but at least since she had turned thirty. At the age of thirty-one she had been ripped from her home in the tiny village of Dámóc, Hungary, forced into a ghetto with her family, and eventually transported to three concentration camps until her liberation—as her family's sole survivor of World War II. She had lost everyone she loved, even her sister Laura, who had survived two of the camps with her, but succumbed to typhus only two months before her freedom in 1945.

After spending a fateful four years in a displaced persons camp on her own, she took me, the child she had borne there, and immigrated to Springfield, Massachusetts, where she remained for the rest of her life. It was not a coincidence that all of her previous moves were forced, never of her own volition.

Through it all, my mother and I had been bound together like needle and thread, or a seam that holds two pieces of a garment together. She pushed the needle to create the most beautiful, head-turning garments and I was the embodiment of her threaded designs. However, despite our undeniable yet sometimes tenuous bond, we were not really alone. A close-knit community had surrounded us and helped us acclimate to a new world after our arrival in America. I wondered what my life would be like, now that my mother and I were truly on our own, with no other family or support system to help us manage our way in the world.

Would we continue to maintain our pattern of disconnected, secretive behavior, the one we had exhibited together during our first decade in America? Or would our move allow us to alter our previously closed-off communication and create a fresh spirit of openness and mutual trust? Although I was sure my mother hoped to continue the behavior pattern she had imposed before our move, I not only dreamed of a whole new altered relationship with her—a dream that relentlessly permeated my thoughts—but I also began imagining an alternative reality of what her life would have been without me in it.

CHAPTER 2

The New Fabrics

> It would be impossible to enumerate all the new fabrics, let alone describe them. They may consist of 100% synthetics (often a blend of several) or of a blend of man-made and natural fibers ... They are almost always crease and shrink resistant ... There is, of course, a reverse side to the picture. The new fabrics, and the old ones treated with the new finishes, are not as pliant or absorbent, and are resistant to shaping, often even to pins and needles ...
> — "Fabrics," page 68

Inconveniently, I reached my full height at the time of our move to Forest Park, when I was entering the eighth grade. The previous year, when I attended seventh grade at Chestnut Junior High in the North End, I was only five feet one inch tall and could remain rather inconspicuous among my peers. In the ensuing year, however, I soared to five feet eight inches, never to grow again.

I had surpassed all my friends from Osgood Street by several inches and did not look forward to attending my new school, Forest Park Junior High School, where I was certain the undoubtedly much shorter students would mock me. I was not wrong. My matriculation at Forest Park Junior High drew little positive attention.

"Hey, Banana Peelstein, how's the air up there?" a boy shouted while walking past me in the school hallway.
"You'll never know, Tim," I responded under my breath.

"I never saw a beanpole as high as you," the same boy added.

"You've probably never been on a farm either," I again snorted to myself.

To add to my insecurities, I noticed that one girl in my class had a posse of fellow female students that walked in a large pack behind her in the hallways, in the cafeteria, or on school grounds during recess or after school. I noted that her followers were similar to a flock of birds, gliding after their leader's every move and maneuver in the strict formation of a murmuration. I could hear their high-pitched chirping and giggling as they flew past me.

As I was so new to the school and the neighborhood, I was not sure what the reason could be for this strange phenomenon, which must have begun in the seventh grade before I arrived. It made no sense to me, yet I desperately wanted to be a part of it. I endured eighth grade, trying to determine how I could penetrate this tight-knit group. If only I could be part of the nest, then I would be accepted into my new school despite the disadvantage of my ungainly height. But I never had the nerve to approach any of the followers to see if I could break into this firmly woven arrangement. I eventually made a number of friends and acquaintances at Forest Park Junior High, but I had to endure the sight of this devoted throng behind their fearless, supremely confident leader every day until ninth grade graduation.

My mother rarely asked me how school had gone. She appeared to assume that my academic life was my business, but how I looked was hers.

"So, Hani, vhat kind of clothes vould you like to vear for your school?" she asked, referring to me by the new diminution of my name. I had graduated from "Hanele" to

"Hani." "I tink some vool skirts mit sveaters vould be nice. Vhen ve make da skirts, ve can go to Casual Corner to look for matching sveaters," she added.

I was excited to take excursions to Casual Corner, a specialty store downtown, which was our splurge when we needed matching items to our homemade clothes, like sweaters and purses. "Sure, Ma. Those wool skirts go well with knit sweaters and knee socks. Can you make them in different colors and prints, like plaid, and maybe some that are pleated? That should do it."

"Yeh, an ve can make some nice sleeveless dresses too dat you can vear on da veekend," she said, already planning her sewing agenda.

Actually, since I had reached my full height at such a young age, my wardrobe began to be so abundant that we could not possibly keep all the creations for very long. We made regular donations to charities and neighbors, who appreciated the exquisite one-of-a kind fashions.

The Pfaff sewing machine, which my mother had received from a fellow Holocaust survivor when the Köhler she had brought with her to America ceased to work, was in a constant whir. It was a sound to which my ears had grown accustomed, as natural as the purported swerving of invisible atoms and the daily rotation of the earth.

Outside of school, my life was totally different. Cherished by my mother, who admired my height, I wore the most beautiful outfits, handmade for me to display her inspired handiwork. My mother and I were sure that the neighbors were watching closely in order to see what homemade outfit I was wearing daily. I could not help but think I was quite special—even elite—at least in my neighborhood community.

I was the odd person "out" at school, despite my pretty attire, but fashionably "in" at home. These confused messages set the stage for a dueling set of self-images that were in constant discord.

*The Pfaff sewing machine, head inverted,
now used as a family photo location*

CHAPTER 3

Basting

> Essentially, basting means temporary sewing, done with long, loose stitches, and removed after a job is completed. Nowadays it is often done by machine ... Its usual purpose is to hold two or more layers of fabric together preparatory to stitching. In modern sewing, this is done whenever possible with pins only. ... Pin-basting may serve by itself or it may be a preliminary to thread-basting. The position of the pins depends on whether your basting is a preparation for sewing or for fitting. —"Basting," page 19

1961 Like all Springfield ninth graders, when I was thirteen and one of the youngest students in my class at Forest Park Junior High School, I had to choose the high school I wished to attend the following year. Based on my vision for my future, I could opt for a trade school, a technical institution, a commerce high school, or a school specifically aimed at training students for their college careers, with a curriculum rooted in the classics. Since my mother had told me repeatedly since I was five that I was destined for college, I chose Classical High School because of its college-bound curriculum and because my mother would not have approved of any other choice.

As a fourteen-year-old freshman at Classical, I was exposed for the first time to a diverse student body from all areas of the city. Early in tenth grade, I invited one of my new high school friends to my house to spend some time together. We soon found ourselves taking a walk through nearby Forest Park, the noted Frederick Law Olmsted-designed stretch of greenery, gardens, lakes, zoo, and sports venues, sliding our feet through the multicolored autumn leaves, which covered the ground beneath us.

As we passed by one of the park's abounding gardens, Joanie and I began to ask each other questions about things we liked to do, friends we had in common, boys we liked best at school, and about our families. Aside from Jane and Mandy, the sisters whom I had befriended when I was in the seventh grade at Chestnut Junior High, Joanie was one of the few new friends that I had attempted to cultivate, not one of those that I had known among my immigrant community.

Joanie spoke freely about her close relationship with her parents. Her stories about trips they had taken, games they had played together, lessons they had taught her, and the generally congenial bond she shared with them enthralled me. Her experience seemed so unlike mine. Having lived with only my solemn mother up to that point in my life, I could not identify with anyone who lived in what I considered a real family.

When we stopped at the playground to sit on the swings, I wiped off the dirt and leaves from my swing before I sat on it with my new cotton lilac pedal pushers and matching short-sleeved shirt and sweater. As we swung, Joanie spoke of the times her father had taken her to the park and gently pushed her on the swings.

> "That was always so much fun. Did your father do that, too?" she asked.
>
> "No."

I responded with just one word, unable to say that my father did not do that because he was never in my life. He had never pushed me on the swings, nor taken me to a ball game, restaurant, or car ride, or kissed me goodnight. He was nonexistent for me. I could not utter any of those words to my new friend. I could not add anything to "no." It was suddenly obvious to me that I had never rehearsed an adequate response to questions about my father. I had left myself totally unprepared.

"What kinds of things do you do with your father?" Joanie asked.

Like a politician, who never directly responds to a question, I pivoted to a guessing game that might allow me to ease into my answer. "Joanie," I said," I have to tell you about something I don't have. Why don't you try to guess what it is and I'll tell you when you're right?"

"Okay," Joanie said, willingly.

I had never participated in such a cryptic dialogue before. I knew why I had decided to deflect the question but I had no idea why I had chosen this uncomfortable game show parody to do so. Still, my subconscious had compelled me to initiate it and Joanie seemed game to play along.

"Uh, is it a TV set?" she asked.

"No, that's not it."

"Is it a car?"

"No, we have a car."

Many more inane questions and answers ensued over the next half hour until finally, I became so frustrated with myself that I decided to get to the crux of the matter. "I'll give you a hint. It's human," I told her, relieved that I had put a stop to this maddening line of questioning, which, I reminded myself, I had started.

"Okay, is it a brother or sister?"

"Well, it's true that I don't have either, but that's not it."

She looked at me rather quizzically, her face turning

ashen. "It must be a father, then," she whispered. "You don't have a father."

"Yes, you're right. You've guessed it. I don't, but I didn't want to stop you from talking about yours. He sounds like a really nice man."

"Yeah, I really look up to him. I'm so sorry for you."

Looking down at the ground, I replied in a muted voice, "Thanks."

That was the end of our conversation about fathers or the absence of them. We moved on to other adolescent subjects and never returned to that line of conversation again during our long friendship. Still, that experience always remained in my mind. Not since an incident when I was ten, when in a game of one-upmanship my friend Irma had blurted out that she had a father and I did not, had I truly realized how deep the wound ached. This time, I was four years older and I no longer needed to call my mother in tears to rescue me from the blow. In fact, I never told her about this incident.

Without my full realization, my mother's secretive behavior, which prohibited any questions about the circumstances of my birth, had repressed my ability to speak aloud with anyone about my absent parent, at least up to that point in my life. Growing up in a one-parent household was not as common in those days as it is today, especially in the Jewish community. To the outside world, my mother must have presented an aura of strict secrecy about the father of her child and the reasons for her single living condition. Not one person had ever asked me about my father, neither among my *grine* community nor among my school friends, as though they all understood that the question was forbidden. Although thankful that I never overtly encountered their curiosity, I was also left unprepared to respond to Joanie's question.

I was missing other close family members, like grandparents, aunts, uncles, and first cousins, as well. I did not possess a single photograph of any of my ancestors—Uncle Dezso, or Aunt Laura, or my grandfather, Simon—that I could show someone and say, "See, that was my family." Even if photographs had existed at one time, my mother could take no remnants of her Hungarian home when she came to America. As I grew older, I realized that an unexplained absent parent—and a totally missing family—would have caused even more speculation and stigma, especially among my peers outside of *di grine*. Like my mother, I kept my silence.

So "father" was a word that I seldom uttered. It never easily rolled off my tongue. Even when I was referring to another person's father, like Joanie's, I struggled to say it. I wished that my mother could offer me some assistance in dealing with the issue, but I knew that was not possible. The deep-seated scar on my unconscious was beginning to emerge.

At the same time, I vowed to never evoke pity from anyone about it, the kind of pity that Joanie innocently expressed when she said, "I'm so sorry for you." That sentence, when referring to me, has always been anathema. My mother had taught me, by example, to always stand up straight, with my head held high and my chin stretched upward. I learned to avoid any pity whenever possible. More importantly, I learned to be much better prepared regarding the "father" question in the future.

CHAPTER 4

Hand-Sewing

> You can be a first class dressmaker these days and not know how to sew a fine seam ... (that's what sewing machines are for) .... Still, you must know how to handle a needle and thread competently. Careful hand-finishing ... will give a garment an expensive look ... How you hold your work will depend on what you are doing.
> —"Hand-Sewing," pages 96–97

I have never been very agile or quick with my hands. At certain times, I toyed with needlepoint and knitting, but I rarely produced anything worth wearing or showing to the public. Musical instruments, such as violin, guitar, and piano, all entered my life at various points, but my lack of manual dexterity reared its ugly head, so these instruments eventually went by the wayside.

Sewing has always been out of the question for me, due to my lack of nimbleness and skill, lack of proper hand and eye coordination, and lack of curiosity. Most of all, as the child of a dressmaking and design master, I had my own personal seamstress at my side throughout much of my life. Why struggle to develop any sewing skill when there was no need? My task was only to serve as the model for my mother's clothing designs, not to be the creator. What's more, my mother never gave me lessons in the art and craft of sewing. At the same time, it was also true that I never asked her to teach me. I was perfectly content to remain in the dark about how needle and thread could be used to construct such beautiful attire.

There was one notable exception to my consistent absence of manual talent: tweezing. Yes, tweezing. When I was fourteen years old and living on Maryland Street, my neighbor, Mrs. Lott, a former fellow tenant and member of *di grine* from our old Osgood Street apartment building, crossed the street to ask me an unexpected question. When I was younger, she and I used to walk to the North End post office together to send the packages she prepared for the Polish family who had saved her own family during the war.

"Chanele (an endearment of my Hebrew name, pronounced with a guttural, throaty sound at the beginning), I alvays look at your eyebrows for a long time. I am vondering if you can tveeze my eyebrows just like yours," she asked, looking intently at my face.

After pausing for a few seconds, I said, "Mrs. Lott, just so I get this straight. You want meee (pointing to my chest) to tweeze yoour (pointing to her chest) eyebrows? You mean with tweezers?"

"Of course, vhy not? I vill come to you and bring my own tveezers."

Before I responded, I gazed down closely at Mrs. Lott's perfectly round face as a whole and then focused only on her eyebrows. Her brows were rather short and dark, matching her jet-black hair, and held a medium high arch in the shape of a crescent moon. I was instantly confident, although I could not explain why, that I could manage pruning them. As eyebrows go, these looked relatively easy to pluck. They seemed ideal to showcase my heretofore hidden manual dexterity.

So I replied, "Uhm … uh, okay, sure, yes, wow, sounds good. I'd be glad to do it."

"It's a deal," she responded, with a gleam in her eye.

After Mrs. Lott asked me this momentous question, I wondered why I had said yes. I did not reveal to her that I had never plucked an eyebrow in my life. I had never even picked up a pair of tweezers. I had no experience as an esthetician whatsoever nor had I ever felt the desire to learn the trade. Not only had I never tweezed or shaped my own eyebrows, I rarely employed any beauty regimen. My mother, ever the aficionado with a pair of scissors, even trimmed my toenails every month with a pair of small nail scissors, as intently as though she were hand-sewing a new garment hem, while I barely looked down at her work.

Soon after Mrs. Lott's departure, my mother, who overheard the conversation, asked, "Hani, I so surprised dat you say yes to Mrs. Lott about tveezing her eyebrows. Do you really vant to do it? I can't believe it."

"Yes, Ma, I really want to do it. I'm not exactly sure why, but I think I can do a good job."

"Okay, Hani. Do vhat you vant," she shrugged in her typical coy manner. "If she don't like your vork den she von't ask you again. Dat's it."

As it turned out, Mrs. Lott loved my meticulous work. Looking at her brows in a hand mirror after each tweezing session, she always commented, "Dey look so beautiful, Chanele. Just right." I could not stop my face from grinning.

Grooming Mrs. Lott's eyebrows eventually became a monthly tradition, continuing until my college years when I was no longer home frequently enough to shape her brows on a timely basis. Even then, I was able to fit in a tweezing now and then. She always gave me a special smile, seeming proud of her neatly pruned eyebrows, when I saw her on holidays at our new Forest Park area synagogue, Kesser Israel, an orthodox *shul* that took the place of the old B'nai

Israel in the North End, as most of its members had moved away.

At last, I had found something I could proficiently do with my hands. Moreover, as I must have instinctively known, I received great fulfillment out of this mundane task. As time went on, I learned how to effectively hold the tweezers to get the best results. It was not until I ceased providing the service that I realized that my unusual elation about this task meant that I had proven my worth as a handicrafter, albeit in a rather odd manner.

My mother was surprised that I had not only exhibited the skill to groom someone's eyebrows, but I had continued doing it for several years to such positive reviews.

> "You doing such a good job on Mrs. Lott's eyebrows, Hani. She seem to like it," she said, after viewing Mrs. Lott's reaction to my work.
>
> "I somehow knew that I could do the tweezing job, Ma. I guess I was right. I'm glad I could make her happy."
>
> "Yeh, she really like it," she repeated and scrunched down one of her eyebrows, as though bewildered at the thought.

I asked myself whether she was really pleased that I had exhibited previously unseen manual agility. Most likely, though, she was unnerved by the possibility that I might eventually become a practicing beautician rather than the college-educated professional she had always planned for. Per usual, she was so inscrutable that I was never certain.

CHAPTER 5

Bonded Fabrics

> These consist of a face-fabric fused to a backing fabric. This generally makes a backing unnecessary and ensures that a garment will keep its shape through dry-cleaning or washing ... Bonded fabrics are gaining so rapidly in popularity and scope that the face-fabric may now be woven or knitted out of practically any fiber or blend. — "Fabric," page 72

I have found it difficult to recall activities that I shared with my mother when we lived together during my adolescence and early adulthood. My memory appeared to be vacant regarding our activities, perhaps due to the sheer lack of them. Our life seemed to revolve around planning and displaying her designs, including trips to purchase patterns, fabric, and notions, and my continuous fittings of garments at various stages of completion. We never played games, such as dominoes, cards, any kind of board game, or even attended a movie, although I always wished we would. She told me that in her youth, she was an expert domino player, which made our non-participation sting even worse. She seemed averse to the pursuit of fun as though it were too entertaining to fit into her sober existence.

We did not travel very much. Although we had spent our first vacation when I was eleven joining a group of *grine* for a week at a resort in Moodus, Connecticut, we relied on others to transport us. When my mother purchased her first car in 1961, we used it mainly to shop for food, clothing, accessories for her creations, and sewing supplies. Later, when I was in high school, we took our longest trips in the Chevy Impala, seventy-five mile drives to New London, Connecticut's Ocean Beach during the summers for occasional beach days. Sometimes, we would stay overnight, renting a room in a rooming house along with other members of *di grine*, a popular and inexpensive way to vacation in those days.

A group of grine in front of their Ocean Beach rooming house. The author is at the far left, Sidonia at the far right.

However, the excursions I remembered the most were those to various banks in downtown Springfield. It felt like we found ourselves in a bank almost once a week. Springfield Institution for Savings and Hampden Savings Bank were well-appointed, majestic venues, marked by a quiet hush of voices at tellers' windows or at managers' desks. Introduced to the banks at a very young age, I was accustomed to their ambience by the time I was a teenager.

My mother liked to diversify her rather meager finances, placing them not into stocks, bonds, or other investment platforms but into multiple banks. She considered those other investments to be too risky. Although the rate of return, in the form of interest, was rather low, she was secure in knowing her money was in bonded, safe hands. She religiously followed the interest rates as avidly as a fan followed the batting average of a favorite baseball slugger. Interestingly, while I always observed her depositing funds, she never seemed to withdraw any. For a long time, I did not even know we could withdraw funds from our savings.

> "See, Hani, ve have five dollars to make a deposit today. Remember, I gave you da bankbook ve use to show to da teller. An you know vhich tellers I like," she would advise me as we entered the building.
>
> "Yes, Ma. I know which tellers here are your favorites. I'll show you the bankbook as soon as they update the balance."
>
> "Tank you, Hani. You know, sometime dey make a mistake mit da interest, so I have to check." And sometimes she was right.

She seemed to gain great satisfaction and even a feeling of exhilaration when depositing even a few dollars into her savings accounts. It must have given her a sense of immense gratification that a "voman alone," an immigrant, could save a little bit of money in America. Her feeling of economic security, although in reality tenuous at times, was her form of self-verification. To be sure, the pride she acquired through those weekly visits easily made the bank trips her favorite excursions. Today's mobile banking options would never have taken the place of her in-person bank pilgrimages. Later, she opened up checking accounts with ATM access (which she never used) at these banks and added Valley Bank, Sovereign, and BankNorth to her diversified list of banking outlets, which safeguarded and protected her small bounty.

CHAPTER 6

Darts

> Darts are stitched, pointed tucks that shape the fabric to fit the body... Since their exact length, depth, and placement have a great bearing on the fit of a garment, they may need some alteration ... First press line of stitching as is, but be careful not to put a crease into fabric by pressing beyond point. Then open out garment, to maintain shaping, complete pressing over a pressing hem ... Trimmed or slashed darts are pressed open like a seam.
> —"Darts," pages 55–56

It was an unusually warm late November day in Western Massachusetts. The temperature promised to be in the low 60s in the afternoon and we expected no precipitation. As usual, a raucous card game of "Pitch," a High, Low, Jack, and Game contest offering daily afternoon diversion, was waiting for me after school. I wondered that morning whether my friends and I could play the game outside on someone's porch or lawn on that balmy day.

As a sixteen-year-old senior at Classical High School, I prided myself on rarely bringing a book home after school. I tried to complete my homework assignments during the course of the school day as often as possible. My mother never asked me about my homework or offered to help me with it. The language barrier and her lack of an education beyond the sixth grade in her home country made her hesitate to help me with my homework. I was on my own when it came to decisions about how to complete my academic assignments.

If she had been more acquainted with and confident about her proficiency in English, social studies, and French, I might not have gotten away with this lax behavior. Although I observed her reading the newspaper from front to back every day, I was not sure that she actually understood every word. Writing and spelling in English had always been a struggle for her. She was much more of a math whiz than I, but she still reneged on any interference with my studies. As always, she just trusted me to do well in school and keep my eyes on the college prize. However, I did not fool myself. She was watching me. If my grades had slipped in any way, she would have made her anger and disappointment known.

Study hall was near the top of my list of favorite classes. Our regular study hall teacher, Mr. Girr, a member of the school's English department, was out that Friday so a substitute teacher, a man I had never seen before, whose name I cannot recall, but whose face I seem to remember better than any other teacher that year, took over the class.

I remember sitting in the front row of the classroom, wearing a homemade brown wool tweed straight skirt, white cotton blouse and brown-flecked wool cardigan sweater that day. The old circular clock high up on the front wall showed a few minutes past 1:30 p.m. in its Roman numerals when the substitute walked quickly out and then back into the room. While I was diligently working on my math homework, he walked briskly up to the front of the classroom and nervously cleared his throat. As I gazed at his glum, somewhat bewildered face, I wondered what this stranger had to say to the students in the class.

"Ahem, can I have your attention please, everyone? I have terrible news. President Kennedy has been shot in Dallas. I wish I had more to tell you but that's all I know right now. As soon as I get more information, I'll give you an update," he loudly announced. Then, just as quickly, he walked out of the room again, presumably to get more information about the shocking occurrence. He must have been quite unnerved at finding himself in a classroom of unfamiliar students, obliged to tell them the shocking news that the president had been shot.

The students in the classroom were silent at first. I turned around to see that everyone was still seated at his or her desk. Although we had all stopped doing our homework immediately after hearing the news, no one could find the right words to talk about what we had just heard. Three girls in the back of the room were quietly sobbing and holding hands, and the boy behind me, who had been soundly asleep before the announcement, was sitting straight up and alert. We somehow remained still, except for the quiet murmur of voices either talking to themselves or to a nearby student. It seemed like an eternity until the unnerved substitute returned to the front of the class to tell us that the president had died of his wounds and school would immediately be dismissed.

As I went back in a daze to my homeroom and then to my locker to retrieve my coat, my heart racing faster than I had ever experienced, I observed students in the hallway finally displaying their emotions about the shocking events. Some students were wailing and wondering aloud about what would happen to the country now that our president had been shot and killed. Kennedy, our former home state senator, had been so young, handsome, and cultured—the ideal politician for our baby boom generation. His sudden, senseless death was hard to comprehend. We wondered whether more shootings would follow. Were any of us safe now? The hallways at Classical High School were a bed of confusion, disarray, and disbelief in the immediate aftermath of that fateful, brutal event. My earlier anticipation of our after-school game of Pitch had vanished as quickly as a speck of dust in a whispering wind.

My longtime friend Sally and I had agreed that morning that rather than taking the city bus, we would get a ride home from my mother. We took the twenty-minute walk down State Street to Main Street and then to William Street in the South End to arrive at my mother's place of employment, the Victoria Dress Corporation, which we usually referred to as "the shop." It was a walk we had taken many times before, but never under such awful circumstances.

Walking down the usually busy State Street, one of the main arteries of the city, was an eerie and grim experience. Other than the students, almost no one appeared on the street, neither in the stores and businesses nor on the road. Strangely, the skies seemed gloomier and the air chillier than they had felt in the morning. We passed by one of our favorite shops, the record store, where we had once met "Old Cape Cod" singer Patti Page and excitedly obtained her autograph. Now the same shop appeared dark and forlorn. It was as though everything had been long planned as a holiday rather than hastily closed in less than an hour. Our world had changed dramatically in what amounted to just a few moments.

We talked about how unreal the scene was as we made our way down the street. "It looks like a ghost town here," Sally tearfully mourned. "I feel so awful about President Kennedy. How can such a thing happen?"

"I never thought it could. It never even crossed my mind," I said, as though we had somehow abruptly crossed a new threshold of maturity, a rite of passage from the innocence of youth to the raw reality of a world that we had heard about from our Holocaust survivor parents, but which we could never quite imagine. It was hard for us to talk the rest of the way to my mother's factory without choking up.

My mother had already come down from the second floor buzz of whirring sewing machines to the first floor of the shop to greet us as we arrived. She and her co-workers had heard the news. Mr. Podell, the company's owner, had announced that the factory would immediately close and urged everyone to head home.

"Hani, ve gonna be alright. Everyting gonna be all right," my mother said to me, with emphasis on the word "all," as we met her downstairs in the bookkeeper's office.

I could see that she was shaken, her eyes glistening with the moistness of recent tears. At the same time, she was trying to hide that from me to allay any worries I might have had about the fate of the country or our own safety. She had been through those emotions of fear and helplessness less than twenty years before in her homeland of Hungary, and then during her time in the camps of the Holocaust. She seemed determined not to allow herself to feel it again.

She continued her attempt to soothe me and Sally, also the progeny of Holocaust survivors, as she drove us home in our cream-colored Chevrolet Impala, our first car, purchased only two years earlier, shortly after she was promoted to forewoman and received a significant salary increase.

"Don't vorry. It's America. It's a shock but da country can vork it out. Don't vorry," she said, still optimistic about her adopted homeland.

We just sat in the back seat, still at a loss for words.

I did not then fully recognize the amount of strength and courage it must have taken for my mother to suppress her own fears that day for the sake of her daughter. After all, her creative production during the Kennedy campaign and his brief tenure as president had been largely based on the fashionable style of his beautiful wife, Jacqueline, and the modern aura presented by the Kennedy family. That style would continue until the end of the 1960s, when my mother wore the perfect pink wool-silk blend dress with hidden seam pockets along with a matching chic single-breasted jacket as the mother-of-the-bride at my wedding.

Sidonia's pink Jacqueline Kennedy-style suit

It seemed strange to say that my mother tried hard to shelter me from experiencing the fear, cruelty, and terror she had endured, since she had regaled me with its bitter details during her regular dinnertime stories throughout my childhood and adolescence, and even later in my adulthood. She needed someone to hear at least some of her horrific wartime experiences—and I was that someone.

Yet those stories, which I began to hear at the age of five, were difficult for me to absorb as actual events as opposed to a series of sad, enrapturing tales. Even though I was unsure about their reality, I knew those events had somehow inflicted great pain on my mother. To me, however, the assassination was incredibly real, perhaps because I was alive when it occurred.

It was only in the moments after I heard about JFK's assassination that I understood my mother's stories were not just sorrowful, enthralling sagas, but actual, real-life events that had changed her life forever, and in turn, mine. Outwardly, I did not break down in tears, but I could never again look at humankind in the same innocent way. The events of the day had shaped my view like the stitched points of a dart on a piece of fabric.

Although my mother had shielded me from many of the evil forces in the world, I now realized that it was a much more complex universe than I had conceived, with real undercurrents and sometimes overt manifestations of iniquity that could erupt at any time. While still believing in the inherent benevolence of the human race, I could also sense the potential for a sinister side that existed beyond my view. My mother could not protect me from that knowledge any longer. Her stories took on greater significance than they had ever assumed in the past. Starting that day, I became more of a skeptic about the people and environment around me.

CHAPTER 7

Train Yourself

> Train yourself to wear a thimble on the middle finger of your sewing hand. You may have been doing without one, but you will find, after an initial feeling of clumsiness, that with this protection you can push the needle forward faster and with much more precision ... Train yourself to stitch at a steady, even pace, even if you have to go slowly. Stitching done in spurts becomes uneven.
> — "Hand-Sewing," page 97
> — "Machine-Stitching," page 117

We did not experience much joy in our household when I was growing up. On the other hand, neither did we endure plunging despair. I guess one could say that we remained at pretty much the same level of emotion during my mother's and my life together—on the low side. Life was quiet, restrained, and largely non-argumentative, with some exceptions when I was an adolescent and we differed on appropriate clothing styles or I had my run of teenage rebellion. At times, I was ashamed of my mother and her vague marital status, her accent, her solitary behavior, and her inability to communicate on a deeper level, leaving me to wonder about things I felt I should know. I knew I was loved, but it was difficult to have a close relationship with someone who was so sober and private.

Yet, she was everything to me. She was often the only person I saw between the time I woke up and when I went to bed at night. I remembered following her around very closely when I was under the age of twelve and we lived in the North End, for fear of losing her. Who else would take care of me?

She never revealed to me the anguish she must have felt every day since World War II changed the course of her life. Her stories of her content home life in Hungary and her terrible Holocaust experiences were enrapturing and sometimes terrifying. I knew I would hear them while eating supper at her kitchen table, a routine that continued even after our move to Forest Park. Because she appeared to have trained herself to be clear-eyed and calm when she conveyed them, I was not sure if the stories were real or some cleverly devised fictional tales. Curiously, though, she spoke very little about the four-year period she had spent at the displaced persons camp where I was born. She may have thought that those remembrances were just too painful to recount in the same unemotional manner.

Lacking joy, we possessed three other qualities instead: pride and determination, and at times, satisfaction. My mother had most of it, but some of it definitely rubbed off on me. She had a grand plan she must have started to develop shortly after arriving in America. She and I had to take life seriously, confidently, and cautiously, especially about whom to trust. Her goal was to capitalize on her design and dressmaking ability and my effective display of her creations to earn recognition from Americans for her creative acumen. She was very strategic when it came to achieving this long-range plan.

While I was not consciously aware as a child of her grand plan and what role I was playing to help her achieve it, I must have sensed it on a visceral level. We were both very serious about playing our roles, and we were equally important to each other. I gave her someone to go through life with and, perhaps more importantly, acted as the model of her exquisite designs. In turn, she gave me the only familial nurturing I would ever have in my early life.

My mother was not much of a disciplinarian. Her rules were more implicit than explicit. Specific punishments for childhood infractions, like those we observed in American culture, such as grounding or time outs, were non-existent for me. But through close observation of her facial expressions, tone of voice, or mood, I understood how to modulate my behavior.

Learning to cook or clean, likewise, was never required. I rarely did either, leaving almost all of it to her. Education and modeling her fashion designs were my main assignments, and she had high expectations regarding both. By the time I was thirteen, she had trained me to stand perfectly straight with my hands by my sides for long periods of time, turning and pausing at just the appropriate moments between each of her pin placements.

"You know vhat I say, Hani. You don't vant a crooked vaistline or a hem, do you?" she warned me countless times, as though I could ever forget to stand up straight. I knew my modeling job very well and intently heeded her training like any intern or apprentice. Life and our work were serious subjects and I rarely questioned them.

As an example, my mother trained me very early on, sometimes by just a look or a shake of her head, that when taking a formal photograph, I must not smile, although occasionally even she broke this rule.

> "Ma, I think I am going to smile when I take my high school graduation photo. Just this once, I think I should show that I'm excited about finally graduating. What do you think?" I asked.
>
> "Hani, vhat, you crazy? You can't smile. You have to show dat you are serious about dis important time in your life. Don't be a *Larifari* (a German word for someone who is nonsensical or insubstantial)."
>
> "Okay, Ma. I promise not to smile."
>
> "Dat's a right, Hani. You smart."

While poring through my photo albums, I notice that I usually followed her direction and did not smile, at least not allowing my teeth to show, when taking a formal photograph. I even see that serious face in my baby pictures.

Although we could sometimes relish a good laugh about a timely topic and some excitement about recognition of her fashions, the inability to feel real joy remained a quality that proved insurmountable for her for the rest of her life—and some of mine. Our internal psyches simply would not allow us to feel it. I sometimes wondered whether some of her experiences during the war as a slave laborer had trained her to remain stoic and unemotional so as to never provoke or inflame her captors to take any brutal action against her. That hardened mode of behavior must have stayed with her well beyond her war years.

An exception could have been her later excitement when her grandchildren were born, extending her family into the future. Otherwise, she had trained herself well to hold her emotions on the inside and to show only pride, soberness, and determination on the outside. I followed suit.

The author as an unsmiling toddler at the Bergen Belsen DP camp

The author as an unsmiling high school graduate

The author as an unsmiling college graduate

CHAPTER 8

Grain in Fabric

> Every woven fabric, no matter what it looks like, consists of lengthwise threads (warp) through which crosswise threads (called woof, weft, or filling) are woven over and under, back and forth ... The *lengthwise* and the *crosswise* grains, therefore, are the direction in which the threads go ... The human figure, like the fabric that clothes it, has two directions at right angles to each other, the perpendicular or "up and down" and the horizontal or "across." — "Grain in Fabric," pages 92–93

As a trained clinical social worker, I know it is not unusual to lack awareness of many of the memories that make their way into the unconscious, as it stores the multitude of events, experiences, behaviors, and emotions that accumulate since infancy. We have no control over the ruminations of our unconscious. Those things are there whether we like them or not.

Until I began to write my memoir, I was not aware that my unconscious had forced my subconscious into a duality, leading me to two seemingly incompatible beliefs: one of superiority and the other inferiority, a not uncommon phenomenon. The totality of all that has occurred in my life has directed me to behave according to one or the other of these beliefs, sometimes even in the same span of time. It explains a great deal about my dichotomous, often baffling nature, dating back to junior high school.

As a child, growing up with my prideful, secretive, independent, yet highly creative mother, I met her need to have just the right person to display her distinctive clothing designs. A tall, slender, fairly attractive girl, I could easily exhibit my mother's voluminous creative designs with a model's flair. Adored by my mother, not only because I was her only family, but also because I was a dutiful and effective partner in her fashion enterprise, I grew to enjoy being the center of her attention and the object of praise and admiration from others, particularly adults. Sometimes I behaved as though I was superior to other girls and women because of my height, my bearing, and most of all, my ability to show off a varied and well-fitting wardrobe.

It took me a long while to crystallize it, but the drive and ambition she instilled allowed me, once I clarified my vision, to eventually excel in my chosen profession, as well as to eventually tell a compelling story about a mother and daughter who willed a life in America. She would not have liked my literary revelations, but she would have applauded my ambition.

Yet, I had this constant, gnawing feeling that I was miserably inadequate. In conversations with my subconscious, I always referred to myself using epithets that were unrepeatable. In an attempt to achieve perfection, not only in my appearance but in all aspects of my life, the same drive to succeed that contributed to my sense of superiority moved me to feel that I had fallen short, and invariably led to a sense of inferiority.

My internal voice always reprimanded me for not attaining the perfect body, free from imperfections and ailments. Nor was I as smart or discerning as many of my peers, I thought, who seemed to possess the innate intellect to solve difficult problems better than I could. Moreover, while I was proud to have been born in a displaced persons camp, a symbol of a better future created from the ashes of human loss and deprivation, I also lamented that I had less worth than an American-born girl. My missing father and lack of a typical nuclear and extended family only added to my self-loathing. These pervasive self-doubts kept me from formulating my life's vision for a long time and allowed my mother's views of my future to cloud my own.

The factor that probably had the most impact on my inferiority complex was undoubtedly the mystery of my conception and birth. Those unanswered questions—how and why I was born and who my father was—haunted me, starting in my adolescence and continuing for the rest of my life. My inability to learn the secrets of my conception led to a sense of failure and guilt that grew incrementally.

At one time, I began thinking that if the idea of my birth had been up to me, I would have stopped it from happening. That way, my mother might have attained her dream of becoming a *"baleboste,"* the Yiddish term usually referring to a proficient housewife, someone married with children and a well-kept home. She would not have borne the incessant shame and guilt of producing a child out of wedlock. This recurring imagining of an alternative reality—of my mother's life without me—began to take shape during my adolescence and continued well into adulthood and even to this day.

To build this alternative universe, I had to first think about my mother's actual life in the years just before her deportation from her little Hungarian town and some of her Holocaust experiences—the history I knew so well from her many mealtime stories. Then, I had to stretch my imagination about some of the events that could have occurred in the aftermath of the Holocaust, when she was confined at the Bergen Belsen displaced persons camp. Finally, I reflected on her long life in Springfield, Massachusetts, and how it could have been different, perhaps more fulfilling in many ways, than her actual existence.

What kind of woman could she have become? How would her

life have evolved? Starting with the familiar true background of my mother's homeland, family life, and Holocaust events, my fantasies began to take up a good portion of my leisure time.

CHAPTER 9

Preparation of Fabric for Cutting

> Pick out pattern pieces you will use (depending on what "View" of garment you have selected on envelope). Smooth out pieces with warm, dry iron. Make pattern alterations, if any. Small pieces, if printed together, must be torn apart. — "Cutting," page 50

Based on my mother's frequent dinnertime stories, I learned a great deal about her earlier life, particularly about the years before she was deported from her hometown and the weeks prior to her journey to a nearby ghetto and then Auschwitz. Combined with my observations of her, those real events set the stage for the imagined occurrences I often wove in my mind. In the years preceding World War II, the real events unfolded this way:

Sidonia was not considered an especially pretty girl nor particularly brilliant. She was darker-skinned than most of her family, possessing a kind of Turkish visage reminiscent of Hungary's Ottoman past, with dark hazel eyes and a widow's peak at the apex of her front hairline. Her looks evoked an aura of mystique. Most people in her village would say she was inordinately clever, creative, and a good tradesperson, adept at diplomatically dealing with vendors about the appropriate price for buying and selling goods brought to markets as part of her family's trading business.

She was born and bred in the northeastern sector of Hungary, along the Czechoslovakian (now Slovakian) border, an area known for its wine, trade, and artisanship. Although she was the youngest sibling in her family, she was taller than any of her three sisters and just a couple inches shorter than her only brother, Dezso. Offsetting her height, her long legs were exceedingly wide and thick, and barely tapered at the ankles.

Like all the women in her family, Sidonia spent much of her days doing farm chores and helping her father in their trading business and other enterprises, including, at different times, a small bowling alley, general store, and tavern. Sewing for the family and for other members of their tiny village was a daily activity, as well.

As a trader and shopkeeper, her father, Simon, interacted with other traders in nearby villages and in larger market towns. In that manner, he was able to obtain precious textiles including new and used fabric, which formed the basis of the clothing items Sidonia and her sisters designed and produced. At times, he also would purchase fabric goods from peddlers who roamed from town to town selling their wares and showcase them in his general store. He was used to being both a buyer and seller of various products.

Their town, called Dámóc [pronounced "Dah-motz"], sat so precariously on the border with Pribenik, a Czechoslovakian village, that depending on the political winds of the time, there were decades during the twentieth century when a part of Dámóc was considered to be Slovakian territory and then reverted back to Hungarian property, seeming to be in a constant state of border fluidity. In fact, since the end of World War I and the dissolution of the Austro-Hungarian Empire, Hungary lost much of its population and land. New borders were created, which proved quite perplexing and inconvenient to those living in border towns. Sidonia and her family considered themselves culturally and linguistically Hungarians, no matter the borders.

By the time Sidonia was thirty, her father, Simon, had still not found a suitable husband for the two youngest of his four daughters, Sidonia and Laura. However, even after the death of their mother and the departures of their siblings, the family continued to lead a contented and fulfilling life in their little corner of the country. As usual, they carried on their trading business as best they could in the tense climate of the country's restrictive laws against Jews.

Simon's wife, Hani (née Klein), to whom he had been married for more than forty years, had died several years earlier after a two-year battle with breast cancer, and one of his daughters, Margit, had succumbed to the Spanish flu pandemic after World War I. At seventy-five, he was happy to have some of his family working along with him, although the lack of potential Jewish spouses continued to frustrate him. At the very least, Simon thought, if he could not find matches for them, he had taught them to live adequately on their own as independent women after he was gone. In addition, he thought they would always have one another and the other members of the large extended Perlstein and Klein families, most of whom lived in the same wine country region and who could serve as a support system for them, if needed.

While Laura attracted a number of men with her light brown hair, blue eyes, and vivacious nature, she never took much notice of them, preferring to wait until her father could find the proper Jewish match for her. Sidonia's plainer looks and sober introspection did not attract men in the same way, but she possessed an air of self-confidence that those around her admired. As I learned in my later adulthood when I secretly read her cache of old letters, Sidonia's lack of male companionship did not mean that she was uninterested in romance or gossip of other young adults and their romantic adventures. She seemed to have had just as many romantic hopes and dreams as any other young woman.

By 1944 they were living during a world war. Even though their country, for the most part, had been spared the horrors of deportation, deprivation, and death at the hands of the Nazis, the family knew that the future for Jews could become dire at any time.

They retained their spirit of optimism, not allowing themselves to be overwhelmed by thoughts that the war could end their life as they knew it. After all, their ancestors had lived in Hungary for at least the previous one hundred and fifty years, tending to vineyards and working as traders, small business owners, and shopkeepers. Hungary, in their minds, was a civilized nation. They tried to keep their faith that the family could continue to live as patriotic Hungarian citizens.

But in early April 1944, when Sidonia was thirty-one and Laura thirty-two, their optimism was quelled. A neighbor across the street, at the request of the local gendarmes, used his horse and wagon to transport them and the rest of their family away from their home. The other family members at home included their father, their oldest sister Szeren, who had left her arranged marriage and moved back home, and their nephew, Dezso's visiting eight-year-old son, Mordkha.

They made their way to nearby Ricse [pronounced "Rich-eh"], the birthplace of Adolph Zukor, the purported founder of Paramount Pictures and Simon's good pal when they were children, before Zukor departed for America. As Dámóc was such a tiny hamlet, too small to support its own synagogue, Sidonia remembered that the synagogue in Ricse had at one time served as their center for religious services.

They spent no time in Ricse, as a local train immediately transported them to the ghetto in the closest big city, Sátoraljaújhely, to await their unknown fate. Any illusions that they may have been spared the same horrors as other Jews in Europe—although it was unclear whether they had known the full scope of the Nazi effort to annihilate all Jews—were effectively gone.

I have read that when Sidonia and her family arrived, the ghetto in Sátoraljaújhely, referred to as Ujhely [pronounced "ooyheh-y-ih"] for short, was already crowded with Jews wrenched from cities and villages in Zemplén County. Within just four days in April 1944, the Hungarian gendarmes had transported all the Jews in the entire county to the ghetto.

About a dozen streets in the gypsy suburb of the city were fenced in and designated to temporarily house the estimated eleven to fourteen thousand individuals who would suffer the degradation and humiliation of distressed conditions in the ghetto, not knowing their ultimate fate. Yet, it seemed that the Hungarian authorities knew and were satisfied all along that the Jews' stay in the ghetto was only "temporary," just a holding place for their eventual deportation to a location outside of their country. Hungary then could go back to its previous status, but be rid of its Jews.

My mother told me that she felt fortunate that some of her relatives, like her sister Etel and her family, lived in Ujhely and would take in the newly arrived family members. Sidonia soon discovered that, due to the lack of living space for all those forced into the ghetto, Etel's small apartment was shared by at least thirty other souls.

Since their roundup had occurred during the last days of the Jewish holiday of Passover, when Jews all over the world celebrated their deliverance from slavery in ancient Egypt, it was especially ironic that the same holiday would mark the reverse—their heartbreaking removal from their homes to a captive environment. To boost their spirits, as he had prepared for the Passover holiday before he left, Sidonia's Uncle Shayme, Simon's brother, who knew many of the ghetto's officials and soldiers, arranged for one of them to fetch his prepared Passover food from his village home. Upon its delivery, he shared his Kosher for Passover bounty with as many people as possible in their overcrowded quarters.

In that tiny apartment, Sidonia reunited with her good friend Kis [pronounced "Keesh"] Etu, Little Etel, stepdaughter of Sidonia's sister, Nady [pronounced "Nod" with a slight "y" sound at the end] Etu or Big Etel. They did not often have a chance to see one another before the opening of the ghetto and relished talking about who else was in Ujhely, catching up on friends and acquaintances who shared their doomed circumstances.

Not knowing very much about the family's time in the ghetto, I always imagined that the Perlstein sisters' reputations as dressmakers would have been recognized throughout the rural villages of the county. It was easy to surmise that Sidonia and her sisters would soon have been asked to use their skills to serve as tailors for their Nazi and Hungarian overseers and officials. They were surely singled out to assist with machine and hand sewing to assure that the uniforms and suits of the numerous Nazi armed forces and Hungarian officials, who administered the ghetto with a tight fist, were in the finest condition.

In following this thread of thought, I imagined their time there like this:

While their overseers' attire remained as tailored as possible, the sisters existed in dire straits, with minimal food, sanitation, and health facilities, their own clothing becoming ragged and soaked with the stench of sweat, soil, and stress. An inadequate water supply and sewage system, along with the inevitable vermin and disease that accompanied these scarcities, plagued the sisters. Yet they continued their labor to keep the officials in their sartorial splendor.

A Singer sewing machine in Etel's small apartment was commandeered and used in rotation to keep up with the demand, not only by Nazi officers and Hungarian gendarmes but local bureaucrats, who included the administrative heads, sub-prefects, mayors, deputy mayors, and registrars of the cities and villages in the northeastern sector of the country, along with representatives of the

Ministries of Interior and Finance. All of them were well aware of the sad plight of those in the "temporary" Jewish quarter of Ujhely.

Sidonia wondered what would happen to their home and valuables, their kitchen and bedroom furniture, and especially their dachshund, Apsi, who remained quietly weeping on a front doorstep of their home as the assigned neighbor took them away from Dámóc. She realized that if they ever returned to their home, it would not be the same way they had left it. Chances were, their belongings had been confiscated, if not by the government, then by their fellow villagers, who must have come to the realization that they would never return. Their animals—Apsi, Cocan the cow, and various geese, hens, roosters, and other farm animals—might have been sold at auction.

She could not bear the thought of losing her home, yet she was also heartened by her family's decision to hide their treasured jewelry behind a stone in the kitchen hearth on the eve of their departure. Surely no one else would find them hidden there. If they ever did return, she was sure the engagement and wedding rings, earrings, tie tacks, pocket watches, and even a few rubles and dollars in that little metal box would comfort them.

Nazi officers, policemen, and gendarmes' uniforms, men's business suits, and women's dresses, owned by the officials' girlfriends and wives, made a steady stream into Etel's apartment for mending and alterations. All assignments were accomplished without any fittings, since the customers, especially the females, feared stepping foot into the squalid ghetto. It seemed new clientele was more than satisfied with the work, judging by the continued requests.

The sisters were kept busy from dawn until dusk and beyond with their sewing tasks. Sidonia was comforted that their talent with needle and thread kept them distracted from their wretched situation. Occasionally, their overseers would reward the sisters with extra rations for their service, while not allowing any of the

*other inhabitants of their quarters the same so-called "privilege."
For the most part, however, they lived on subsistence fare, barely
enough to nourish their bodies.*

*As they toiled in the ghetto's horrible conditions, they were
bone weary at the end of each day. Often hungry and light-headed,
Sidonia wondered if she would be able to rise up early each
morning to resume work. After six weeks or so, however, Sidonia no
longer had to worry about the daily grind of clothing alterations for
their brutal captors. She had a harsh awakening.*

TOWARD MID-MAY, 1944, when the family would traditionally prepare for Shavuot, commemorating God's gift of the Torah to the Israelites, they observed the line of cattle railcars coming to a screeching halt in Ujhely. The Perlstein family was among the first to board.

While the urbane Swedish diplomat Raoul Wallenberg would valiantly save thousands of Hungarian lives in Budapest with his Swedish passports and safe houses, he could not save the Jews in the Ujhely ghetto nor others in the ghettos of the countryside, who were herded onto trains headed for the Auschwitz death camp. The Perlsteins comprised only a tiny fraction of the close to 440,000 Hungarians across the country who were deported in the last full year of the war, even as the Nazis suspected their own defeat, to meet their bleak destiny in a mere seven-week period of time.

CHAPTER 10

Patterns

> American dress patterns are probably the most carefully designed, accurately drafted anywhere. Patterns, however, are not cut to exact measurements. This would produce skin-tight garments, entirely unbearable. A considerable allowance (ease), especially in the width, must be added for the wearer's comfort and freedom of movement. How much allowance is needed, and how it is distributed, is left to the pattern companies' quite careful discretion ... To dispose of the question of pattern-brand: Here you can only proceed by trial ... Patterns, incidentally, are never returnable to the store. — "Patterns," pages 127–128

As a senior at Classical High School, most of my thoughts were centered on where I would go to college. I saw this as a chance to get far away from my mother and the torture of my inability to communicate with her about things that I thought really mattered. I toyed with the idea of choosing a college in California and asked my guidance counselor to explore possibilities on the West Coast. Yet, in the end, I could not bear the thought of being so far away from her. I only applied to one school and was luckily accepted at the University of Massachusetts at Amherst, less than an hour away from Springfield.

In the mid-1960s, UMass was a bucolic campus surrounded by rolling hills and upland forests, not too far from the famed Berkshire Mountains in western Massachusetts. The state's flagship university was then on the verge of expanding its residence halls, educational programs, and buildings on campus, and branching out to multiple sites in other parts of the state. The tuition rates were low then and I was fortunate to receive government loans, scholarships from the National Council of Jewish Women, and in my senior year, tuition reimbursement for services as a dormitory counselor, all easing the financial strain on my mother.

The author's UMass freshman ID showing the widest photographic smile the author has ever displayed

I entered as a freshman, just a few days after my seventeenth birthday. I had been away from my mother only once before, when I was eleven and visited my mother's cousin Olga's family in Kansas City for a summer, but this was my first excursion into being truly on my own for an extended period.

Dwight House was my chosen residence hall, a small traditional dormitory in the northeast section of the campus, even then referred to as one of the "old dorms." Barely seventeen, I did not feel ready to live in a larger, more modern residence, like the new high-rise dormitories. As a member of the large influx of baby boomers entering UMass, when the undergraduate student population swelled from six thousand to more than ten thousand, I sought a smaller, more insulated environment, similar to the one I had left at home.

Yet even at Dwight House, I began to realize that most of the in-state students were from the eastern part of our small state, particularly the Boston metropolitan area and Cape Cod. My hometown of Springfield and the rest of Western Massachusetts were much less known and less densely populated. All along I had thought Springfield was the center of the universe, when most of the students barely knew it existed!

The late 1960s at UMass saw the advent of anti-war protests, sit-ins, pot parties, and general student unrest and activism in the wake of the Vietnam War. I participated in a subtle manner, sympathizing with the protests, and occasionally joining fellow students, but playing a somewhat subdued role.

During my years in Amherst, I dated a few students, but had no serious relationships. Despite some brief excesses as a very young freshman newly away from home, I viewed college as not a place to find a husband, but somewhere to learn more about the world and to ultimately attain the skills required for a profession—a profession that remained murky and unidentified throughout my years there. My vision for the future, as it pertained to my profession or marriage and family, was unusually shapeless, unfocused, and almost vacant for most of my early life, no matter how hard I tried to crystallize it.

My mother's relentless urging at an early age that I attend college had been just that. *Go to college.* She was no help in assisting me to focus on the subject or discipline I wanted to study nor the career I wanted to practice. The choice of what I specifically wanted to pursue as my profession appeared to be up to me. Psychology seemed to be an area in which I thought I might do relatively well, although this choice was based on no real research or rationale, and without much attention to career options. In the same vein, once I began my psychology curriculum, I wavered and thought I might prefer a history major instead, but I never acted on my intuition, never achieving the nerve to disrupt the path to psychological uncertainty. The inferior aspect of my unconscious duality started to take over. I continued to lead a distinctly blurred existence for most of my years at UMass.

At times, the superiority feature of my duality quickly gained prominence. As I proceeded through my studies, learning more about abnormal, clinical, and educational psychology, and human genetics, I must have also impressed my fellow students with my beautiful, fashion-conscious wardrobe. This led to my nominations as the Best Dressed Girl on Campus and Military Ball Queen.

Daily Collegian Photo by John Griffin

BEST DRESSED COED—Angel Flight and Glamour magazine are sponsoring jointly a contest to determine the Best Dressed Coed on the UMass campus. The contest will be finalized next Sunday at 2 p.m. in the Ballroom when the winner will be announced. Shown in the picture are: front row: Janine Potvin, Antoinette Antonelli, Claire Dihorati, Susan Bender, Mary Ann Paraskas and Sivia Bartlett; center row: Kathy Lorenz, Andrea Kittay, Linda Pomfrit, Pamela Parsons, Carol Vickers, Suasan Arlenson, Ellen Gassow; back row: Mary Ellen MacKenzie, Maura Smith, Julie Quincy, Lynn O'Connell, Janet Spense, Barbara Ackson, Gail Epstein, Honey Perlstein, and Barbara Nelson. Missing is Clair Dolan.

Best Dressed Girl contestants, from the author's student copy of The Daily Collegian. *The author is in the back row, second from the right.*

Realistically, my chances to be named Military Ball Queen or even selected for her court were doomed. On the day the contestants' photos were taken, my adolescent face broke out in the worst case of acne I had ever experienced. The blown-up poster of my spotted visage, which hung among those of the other nominees in the university's Student Union, beckoning for votes, would haunt me for the rest of my college days, and assuredly squashed any chances for victory.

On the other hand, my odds at winning the Best Dressed Girl competition remained high. I knew that I would likely be the only contestant wearing an entirely homemade wardrobe, and by the time I was a UMass student, I was mostly proud of that fact. My freshman roommates had begun to call me "Honey," a nickname that stayed with me throughout my four years at college, and I was pleased to receive numerous good luck wishes from other students: "We're rooting for you, Honey!"

My mother was elated to learn about the attention I received for the way I looked and dressed at college. The excitement she exhibited in creating the three new garment ensembles for the final festivities of the Best Dressed competition was a huge departure from her usual somber mood.

> "Hani, I so happy dat people at your school like your clothes. I so proud of you," my mother told me when I came home to see her.
>
> "Well, it's all because of you, Ma. Everything I wear is some creation of yours."
>
> "Let's make dis da best clothes ve ever made," she said with conviction, as I stood for what seemed like an eternity for fittings in preparation for the competition.

The outfits she created were an informal soft brown wool tweed skirt and turtleneck sweater, a dressier dark fuchsia wool-silk skirt and long jacket with stand-up collar, and a pink and magenta color-blocked satin ball gown.

I did not win that competition, but came close. My mother joined me for the ceremony, watching me model her special designs with a constant smile on her face. Seeing her so content that day, I gained the most satisfaction I had ever attained in my efforts to please her.

CHAPTER 11

Bias Binding

> Trim away the entire 3/8" seam allowance (since bias strip covers garment edge, no allowance is needed). Before doing this, stay-stitch ¼" from raw edge. — "Bias," page 28

As my mother told the story, upon leaving the ghetto, the Perlsteins took a grueling three-day ride in a rail car with no food or water, crammed in with at least one hundred other desperate souls, some of whom died before their final stop, Auschwitz. Upon arrival, the infamous Dr. Mengele and his cohorts made selections of who would live and who would die. Only Sidonia and Laura were chosen to live. The rest of the family—their father, Simon, their sisters Etel and Szeren, and their nephew Mordkha—were selected for immediate death in the gas chambers, along with seventy-five percent of the other deportees. Sidonia and Laura never again saw them or most of the rest of their extended family, including aunts, uncles, cousins, and stepfamily members. Having lost everyone else they loved, they vowed to stay close together for as long as possible.

The sisters were assigned to the Scheisskommando, the team of inmates in charge of cleaning out the common latrines, thought to be a desirable assignment since the malodorous stench of the latrines made the guards less apt to come close to them. It was also a beneficial meeting place for inmates, where they could talk; sing familiar Hebrew songs; trade scarce camp commodities, like food, clothing, and shoes; or share rumors and observations of camp events.

One time, someone from the male section of the camp, who had resided in a nearby village, spotted them and motioned to them to come close, while taking care not to touch the electrified fence. He told them that he knew their brother, Dezso, and had seen him in the camp, but had lost sight of him. He did not know whether Dezso had died or had been transferred to another camp. It was not much information, but still a welcome piece of knowledge for the sisters, since it meant that their only brother, who had been deported from a different location, might still be alive. Dezso's unknown fate, at the time, was better than the certainty of his death. They hoped that they might someday see him again.

Less than three months later, they were transported westward to the Dachau concentration camp near Munich, arriving on August 1, 1944. It might have been there that Laura and Sidonia began their age deception, when they offered dates of birth of 1914 and 1915 respectively, two years younger than their actual ages. Camp personnel upon arrival interviewed both, where details regarding their description and history were recorded. Some of Sidonia's data included her place of birth, Dámóc; her Dachau prisoner number, 86794; her parents' names; her marital status, unmarried; and a host of other descriptive data, culminating in the date and place of her "arrest" on May 10, 1944, at the ghetto of Sátoraljaújhely.

With the help of the United States Holocaust Memorial Museum's International Tracing service collection, I obtained a copy of my mother's questionnaire and those of Laura and Dezso. Only recently, I noticed that at the bottom of both sisters' questionnaires, the following sardonic statement appeared: "I have been informed that punishment for forgery of documents will occur if the above-mentioned information proves to be false." Underneath this warning, which I translated from the German, the prisoner was supposedly asked to sign her name, attesting to the truth of her statements. As I looked closer, I noticed that the

Sidonia's Dachau questionnaire, courtesy of the ITS Collection, United States Holocaust Memorial Museum

signature on Sidonia's questionnaire was grossly dissimilar to her handwriting. It looked as though she had never actually signed her name to the document, which may have been signed by the person conducting the interview. In light of the circumstances and environment—essentially, captives imprisoned in a labor and death camp—what could have been the punishment for "forgery of documents?"

Their first assignment in Dachau was to join a cadre of female prisoners who performed housekeeping chores at the nearby Schloss or grand castle, recently taken over by the German army, the Wehrmacht. One day, while walking in a small group of women from the camp to the castle, Laura noticed a coat worn by another prisoner. She was sure she had sewn that very coat at home in Hungary and had worn it until she was stripped of her clothes upon arrival at Auschwitz. Although the coat seemed like a mirage, she told the woman she could easily identify it by the Hungarian currency sewn into its interfacing. Presented with the facts and the money uncovered in the interfacing, as Laura predicted, the fellow inmate handed the coat to Laura. Small though the victory was, it was a moment of supreme satisfaction in the most unimaginable place for both sisters.

Later in autumn, the sisters were assigned to a crew handling machine parts for a factory, hidden in a bunker hollowed out of the side of a mountain that manufactured fighter jets for the German Armaments Ministry. They traveled to Kaufering, one of eleven subcamps of Dachau, where they lived in underground earthen huts covered with sod to hide their existence to enemy aircraft. One day, as Sidonia lifted a piece of steel or concrete for transfer to the factory, she dropped the heavy object on her shin and fractured her leg.

Fearing that the accident could lead to her death if the guards noticed she was injured, Sidonia was determined to report to roll call, the *Appell*, the next morning at four o'clock, hoping to somehow hide her fresh injury. A harsh response from the Nazi guards would await anyone who did not report, came late, or could not stand still for the calling of the roll, which could take hours.

She apparently never needed to keep her wound a secret. As luck would have it, the Camp Commandant's voice blared through a loudspeaker at the start of the *Appell*, asking if any prisoners could sew. Despite her shattered leg, Sidonia somehow stepped forward and shouted, "*Ja!*" Of all the women in line who had stepped forward, the guard chose her. From that point onward, she acted as a seamstress for the officers, soldiers, and staff at the camp, working in the headquarters building of one of the Kaufering camps. Allowed to remain seated for the rest of her time as a slave laborer, she was somehow able to hide or at least minimize her injury, which remained untreated.

Sidonia's time during the last few weeks of her detainment at the Dachau subcamp was shrouded in mystery. She never shared whether she worked alone or with other prisoners in her new assignment. Was she the only prisoner chosen that day to work as a seamstress?

She also never revealed the conditions under which she worked as a seamstress or the equipment available to perform the sewing jobs, other than needle and thread. She told me that she used only a needle and thread to insert zippers by hand for the first time in pairs of pants. Although zippers had come into popular use in the 1920s and '30s, they were unknown in her small hometown. She had to call on her sewer's intuition to do the job.

Sidonia knew that her sister could not continue the hard labor on the munitions detail much longer. Many other prisoners at Kaufering died due to inhumane conditions, starvation, and exhaustion, and Sidonia feared that her sister would suffer the same fate unless her conditions were changed as soon as possible. On several occasions, she asked the guard in charge if Laura, prisoner number 86795, could join her as a seamstress. She advised him that her sister was an even better dressmaker than she, and "*Sie könnten eine gute schneiderin gebrauchen,*" she said, using the

German she had learned from her mother. The camp could really use an excellent sewer like Laura.

The reply after some initial investigation was, "No." Laura was needed on the munitions kommando and could not be spared for reassignment to the dressmaking unit, they claimed. However, soon thereafter, the guards changed their minds and Laura was allowed to join Sidonia, sewing for Nazi officials and staff.

The other events of mid-October to mid-December 1944, whether they were consoling or disconcerting, remain forever unknown.

CHAPTER 12

Hidden Button Loop

> Thread loops consist of a core of a few threads covered with blanket stitch ... [a button loop is] an inconspicuous loop usually placed at the neck corner of an opening, often for use with a small button concealed under a collar. Use thread single, bring out at one end of loop-position in a manner that will conceal knot. Across loop-position, take three or four stitches, loose enough to form loop of desired size. Then cover with blanket stitch.
> —"Thread Loops," page 167

In 1965, just as I was entering the spring semester of my freshman year at UMass, my mother received some shocking news. On a visit home, I found her lying in bed in the middle of the afternoon, one arm above her head and the other covering her eyes. She was tossing and turning and muttering to herself, "Mine life is over."

Initially, she was reluctant to tell me the cause of her distress. After probing further, I learned that her boss, Mr. Podell, had decided to retire. He had sold the shop to the foreman, who proceeded to remove her from her forewoman's position, giving her the option of remaining as a sewing machine operator. He knew that her humiliation at this demotion would be overwhelming and that she would refuse. She decided to quit her fourteen-year job, the only one she had known since coming to America.

She asked, "Vhat should I do now, Hani? Oy, I don't know vhat to do. I can't do anyting else but sew."

When the master seamstress asked that question, I could only respond by saying, "You're the best dressmaker in the world, Ma. You should go into your own business. I bet many people would like to wear your beautiful homemade creations, not just me."

After thinking about it for only a few moments, she agreed. In a short amount of time, she opened her own dressmaking enterprise, "Sidonia Perlstein: Dressmaking and Alterations," which went on to grow into a bustling home-based business for years to come. Selfishly, I benefited, too, as her independent venture left her more available to design and create clothes for me as I continued my college studies.

Soon after, during the summer hiatus between my freshman and sophomore years of college, when I was just about to turn eighteen, I unexpectedly came the closest I had ever come to unearthing revelations about my father. Although I had thought about asking my mother so many times during junior high and high school, and wanted to do it so badly, I never even came close to doing so. My hopes of finally being able to confront her when I became an adolescent had been consistently dashed by my own inability to open up a dialogue about the things that we had always repressed.

Sometimes, when we were having a conversation about an innocuous subject, I subconsciously thought that it might have been the right time to slip in a question about her stay at the displaced persons camp and somehow segue into how she had met my father. But my mouth just would not cooperate. I had asked the question directly only once, when I was six and just beginning to realize that our family was different from those around us. As boldly and clearly as only an innocent young child could, and as candidly as I would ever be able to utter it, I asked, "What happened to my father, Ma?" Her firm reply: "I tell you vhen you are sixteen."

Now I was almost eighteen, and she still had not told me.

That summer was just a few months after she transitioned to owning her own design and dressmaking business and began working out of her well-supplied sewing room. It was a distinct contrast to her years of commuting every day to the dress factory, where she sewed dresses for unknown buyers of the company's styles. As I came home that summer, she was in the throes of recruiting customers to her emerging enterprise, desperate to continue making a living, and eager to affirm that she had made the right decision.

Sitting in one of her upholstered living room chairs, she must have been thinking about the work projects for her few new customers while busily doing some hand pinning and stitching on a garment. Although we were not in the midst of a conversation, she wistfully commented that maybe she should have returned to Hungary after the war instead of waiting in the displaced persons camp to come to the United States. "Den maybe I vouldn't meet dat jerk," she blurted without any provocation.

I immediately knew that when she uttered that word, "jerk," she was referring to my father. It must also have been her memories of the "jerk" that had caused her to say, shortly after our move to Forest Park, "Who vants to cook and clean for a man?" Indeed, I never saw her date or become romantically involved with a man. Despite some earlier friendships with a few of the male survivors among *di grine*, along with their wives, she never seemed to show an interest in male companionship. I heard through the grapevine that she had even rebuffed some invitations to go out with some of the single men in our immigrant community. Her shame and guilt regarding her past experience must have been overwhelming.

When she referred to the "jerk," I immediately thought of the mysterious photograph that I had inadvertently seen one day of me, at almost two years of age, and an unidentified person sitting with an arm around my waist, near the displaced persons camp. The photo had been cut to block out the person's face and body, leaving only a part of his or her leg and hands. My head looked as though it had also been cut off at one time, but had been reattached with a piece of tape. Why was the photo so mutilated? Could the person in the missing half of the photo have been the "jerk?"

The mutilated partial photo

It was this unforced disclosure on that summer day that finally made me begin to understand the depth of my mother's vulnerability and sadness about living her life alone. Yet, I still retained a residue of anger at her for depriving me of the knowledge about my conception.

This unexpected, somewhat obtuse conversation with her about my father caused my imagination to really kick in. I began to wonder how my mother's decision-making might have changed had her sister, Laura, lived for a while longer instead of losing her life shortly after her arrival at Bergen Belsen.

In reality, the beautiful Laura had managed to live through the horrible conditions of Auschwitz and Dachau, but was severely debilitated by the time they were transported to the Bergen Belsen camp in December 1944. As Sidonia once told me, "Bergen Belsen vas just a place you go to die." Their sewing skills were of no use to them in the wretched, soul-consuming conditions at Bergen Belsen.

Laura was very close to death when Sidonia brought her to the so-called *Krankenlager* [Sick Camp] in February 1945, hoping some chance might exist for her sister to survive the ravages of typhus. If Laura could receive some treatment, she might be able to recover and resume her place by Sidonia's side. Although Sidonia, herself, also suffered from the disease, as did most of the other 60,000 prisoners by that point, she knew she was stronger both constitutionally and psychologically than her sister and did not worry about herself.

If only Laura could live! Then Sidonia would have somebody of her own, a remnant of her beloved family. She told me she prayed to God as she had never prayed before to let Laura live. She tried to remember the prayer that her family had chanted for the sick during their Shabbat services, sometimes at their Uncle Shayme's large home in Dámóc, when they could not make the trip to Ricse or later to nearby Zemplénagárd to attend synagogue.

"Oh God, have mercy on her and restore her health and strength. Restore her body and spirit. Grant her a *r'fu-ah sh'lei-mah* [a complete and speedy recovery]. *Ba-ruch a-tah A-do-nai, ro-feh ha-cho-lim* [Praise you, Eternal God, the Source of healing and health]."

Sidonia kept repeating her pleas to God over and over while sobbing in her little corner of their overcrowded, lice-ridden bottom bunk. She and Laura had made a solemn promise to each other when they first arrived at Auschwitz and had watched the rest of their family steered to their deaths: they vowed to stay together until their horrible journey was over.

"Please, Lord, please let Laura survive," she pleaded. "She is all I have."

Unlike the reality of Laura's death in the Bergen Belsen concentration camp, in my imagination, against all odds, Sidonia's prayers were answered.

The miracle occurred. Despite no treatment from the camp's hospital, Laura somehow rallied from her extreme illness and returned to the Grosses Frauenlager *[Large Women's Camp], created to accommodate the heavy influx of prisoners moved there from other camps in the east, as Allied forces made their way through former enemy territories. Although still suffering from malnutrition and delusionary episodes, she remained alive there until the British Second Army, 11th Armoured Division, liberated the Bergen Belsen camp on April 15, 1945.*

The long miserable winter at Bergen Belsen was finally over. Sidonia and Laura watched as the British soldiers set about bringing in food and medicine to the survivors and carried out the awful task of burying the 14,000 corpses strewn over the camp's grounds into mass graves. Then they set the diseased camp ablaze.

Sidonia continued to put Laura's life before her own and nursed her back to reasonable health, feeding her small doses of food to prevent any gastric overload after their long period of starvation.

"I alvays try to push Lori before me, even vhen dey gave us our prisoner numbers in da concentration camps. Her number vas alvays right next to mine. An ve alvays share our food. I vanted to protect her vherever ve vere," she once said.

They were soon transferred together to the former Panzer army training camp. A mile and a half away from the Bergen Belsen concentration camp, it had been transformed into the newly designated displaced persons (DP) camp. Located in the Lower Saxony region of Germany, the camp would house 12,000 survivors from many European nations. The sisters shared a room in one of the army barracks with a Hungarian-speaking Romanian woman, with whom they soon bonded.

Sidonia, at left, with friends at the DP camp

At the displaced persons camp, the survivors attempted to regain some semblance of a normal life after the harsh deprivations of the Holocaust. They formed committees for many ventures, such as the promotion of immigration to Israel and the establishment of hospitals, nurseries, schools, and vocational training. When seen in photographs taken at the time, the camp residents looked like *average young people of any community after World War II. As a matter of fact, life at the DP camp seemed full of hope and vitality and a sense of making up for the time that had been robbed from them. Still, loneliness, desolation, and longing for their lost families pervaded the residents' every thought. Laura at first hallucinated about their Hungarian home and family, often calling out family names, sometimes unaware of her actual surroundings.*

In 1946, during the second year of her stay at the displaced persons camp, Sidonia met the young man who would change her life forever. Simcsu [pronounced "Sim-choo"], the sisters' roommate, seemed to know quite a few of the survivors who now walked and biked freely around the displaced persons camp, some of whom she had known in her hometown in Romania. Often dressed in suits, ties and fedora hats, a group of handsome young men, who looked as though they were in their early twenties, walked together as though in a pack.

One day, while Sidonia and Simcsu were out walking on the Lüneburg Heath, where the camp was located, a couple of those handsome men crossed their path. As the men stopped to say hello to Simcsu, she introduced them to Sidonia as brothers who came from her hometown. The younger of the two men seemed to have a gleam in his eye when introduced to Sidonia. He asked her questions in Hungarian about where she was from, with whom she was staying, and what were her hopes for future emigration from the camp. He hoped to meet her again, he told her, for a stroll the next day.

Although she had lied about her age and passed for twenty-seven, Sidonia was actually thirty-three years old in 1946. She had never been alone with a man, as was the norm for single women in her little village, yet she was enchanted by this young man, whose name, he told her, was Samuel Yungman. Although she sensed that he was younger, she was unaware of their actual age gap. Despite her inner warning to proceed with caution, she said yes to his offer of a stroll.

Soon, Sidonia and Samuel began spending consistent time together. While Sidonia remained watchful over Laura's health, she also looked forward to seeing Samuel whenever possible. They were counted, together with Samuel's brother, Eker, in the census of survivors at Bergen Belsen in 1946, part of the list compiled after the war of those who had survived, the "She'erit Hapletah" [Hebrew for the "surviving remnant"]. All their names were listed close together in the count, reflecting their attachment during that time.

Sidonia had begun a liaison with a young and charming man, who made her feel less lonely and despondent. She felt alive again. He seemed to care about her, touched her affectionately, and made her believe that, somehow, there was a future ahead for her.

She waited to introduce him to Laura. Her sister's delicate health meant that those around her were cautious about unduly exacerbating her condition, either mentally or physically. However, Sidonia was finally ready, and was eager to introduce him at last to her sister.

CHAPTER 13

Fabric Belt Loops

> Belt loops are necessary for any belt that is not at the natural waistline; or for keeping a narrow belt in place over a wider waistband. They also serve to keep belts from getting separated from garments. The number of loops needed depends on design and function ... A belt must slide easily through loops. When attaching loops, make sure that there is enough slack. — "Belt Loops," page 22

1968 Graduating from college at the age of twenty was a mixed blessing. I was easily smart enough to keep up with my classmates. That was not a problem. Rabbi Edelman, the principal of my early private religious school, the Lubavitcher Yeshiva, had done me a favor by allowing me to enter the first grade at the age of five. Who can complain about achieving an early start to an education, and therefore, to life? At the same time, however, it also meant that I might not be emotionally mature enough to handle the responsibilities and life decisions that came along with it. My lack of maturity and my hazy vision about my future may have negated the advantage of getting an early start, after all.

As usual, I did not know what I should do after graduation with my Bachelor of Arts degree in Psychology in hand. Strangely, the Harvard University secretarial pool, as they then referred to it, indicated an interest in hiring me after my graduation. I was never sure how they even heard about me since I did not remember ever applying for a clerical position there or anywhere else.

Ironically, although I have always had the utmost respect for administrative assistants, I did not even know how to type, file, take shorthand, or perform any clerical duties, all of which were required. Why would I be interested in a clerical job when I had just received my degree in psychology? Offended that Harvard had stereotypically assumed that, as a woman, I had the experience, skill, and ambition to join their clerical group, I clarified my vision enough to say an emphatic "no."

I felt differently when recruiters from G. Fox & Company, the famed department store in Hartford, Connecticut, came to UMass seeking graduates for their management team. I decided to go for an interview, which went surprisingly well.

"I see here that you were one of the nominees for the Best Dressed Girl on Campus," the recruiter commented, as he read the summary of my college experiences.

"Yes, I wore my mother's homemade fashions to all my classes and activities and also to the final ceremony of the contest. Actually, I've been involved with fashion and modeling my whole life," I replied.

"Well, your grades are very good, although I see you haven't taken any classes in business or management. But with your background, I think you would be an asset to our organization. We purchase women's clothing for sale to our customers and you seem to have the experience we could use. You might eventually want to be one of the buyers for our women's clothing line. How would you like to join our executive training team? You can start right after your graduation."

"I would like that very much. I accept your offer," I said without hesitation. It was that quick.

So, with my foggy view of the future, I thought I would try my hand in a retail setting. My mother's training in the fashion industry may have given me the expertise to help the store in buying for their clothing inventory. With my mother's nod of approval, I began to make the half-hour commute each day from Springfield to Hartford to learn the inner workings of G. Fox & Company.

The store had recently been sold to the May Company, losing its independent status. The rumor was that Beatrice Fox Auerbach, its renowned owner before the sale, still presided over the store. She purportedly had a private office on the top floor. Making it to the top floor to catch a glimpse of Mrs. Auerbach was the intention of everyone on the squad.

Once in one of the store elevators, assuming I was alone, I asked myself how hard could it have been to push the button for the top floor? That action still would not have assured me a sighting and the risk of getting caught and dismissed from the team was just not worth it. Even if the rumor was true, Mrs. Auerbach was already of an advanced age, so we were unsure how often she actually came into the store. Although I thought of every conceivable way to accomplish the feat, I never had an opportunity or an assignment to go to the penthouse floor and achieve the goal of an "Auerbach sighting." Beatrice Fox Auerbach, a true legend in the American business world for her fair labor practices, passed away only a few months after my departure from the store.

I would never forget my summer at G. Fox. It exposed me to every part of a large department store, including women's and men's clothing, women's shoes, hosiery, toys, and the techniques of comparing prices with the competition. The main lesson was to reveal my own ability as an administrator and give me a grasp of teamwork, deadlines, quick decision-making, coordination, public interaction, and budgets. Although I did not realize it at the time, it also helped me take the early steps I needed to shape my dim, shadowy vision of my future ambitions.

I instinctively knew that the world of retail was not right for me. I had a psychology degree and I needed to do something with it. As only a twenty-year-old college graduate, I felt I needed more education before I was permanently tied to a profession.

The following autumn, I left G. Fox and entered the University of Connecticut as a masters candidate in counseling, which seemed like a potentially productive complement to my psychology degree. Although I had also been accepted at New York University, I chose nearby UConn. As much as I said I wanted to leave my mother and move far away from her, each time I had to make that decision, I seemed unable to bring myself to do it. To top it off, in order to save costs, I stayed home with her and drove the one-hour distance each way to Storrs, Connecticut, from Springfield several days a week. It seemed the more I thought I wanted to separate my life from hers, the less I was able to accomplish the task.

My mother didn't try to influence this decision, just as she hadn't with most of the choices I had thus far made in my life: my study habits, my high school selection, my choice for undergraduate school, and my college major. My decision to attend a graduate school closer to home seemed to fall right in line with my mother's desires for me. She did not need to voice her wishes since I seemed to obey them anyway. I was like a belt loop fastened closely to her waistline to prevent any separation from the garment.

My first year of graduate school was also a prolific time for my mother's fashion production. Having me home, except for when I was in Storrs, and available for ongoing fittings allowed her to take advantage of my more mature form as a young woman of twenty-one.

At that time, our reliable source of fabric, patterns, and thread, Osgood Textile, remained on Osgood Street; as the business grew, they eventually moved to larger locations. Despite our move to Forest Park, we had consistently returned there to obtain our discounted sewing supplies and to maintain my mother's long friendship with the owners, Herb and Lillian Kahan. They knew that she could not remain separated from them for too long. Based on her steady sewing production, she needed to constantly replenish her fabrics and notions to accommodate her new fashion ideas for her loyal customers and me. During the year I remained home to work on my first master's degree, I had the opportunity to observe her interactions at the store more frequently than I ever had.

"What are you looking for today, Sidonia? If you let me know, I'm sure I can find it for you right away," said Herb, who stored the location of every bolt of fabric in his head.

"Oh, you know. Just a couple yards of grey vool and some gray rayon lining vill be fine. Let me see vhat you got," my mother responded, already knowing which direction in the store to turn.

"I know what you like, Sidonia. There are a lot of choices here for you to look at. I have a bolt of gray wool right here. Let me get it so you can check out the weight, color, and how it drapes," Herb said, as he carried the bolt to a counter and unrolled a few yards of material.

"Dis is da vool I vant, Herbie," she said, while examining the fabric with her eyes and hands. She was satisfied with its weight, shade, and drape. "Now just da lining to match an I'm all set."

I just looked on as the whole experience unfolded before me. After purchasing a zipper, pattern, and seam binding, we left the store. Our whole visit lasted less than fifteen minutes. Although each visit was relatively short, it was multiplied by an interminable number of trips.

It was the era of linen bell-bottoms and matching tunic tops, of solid color and psychedelic print cotton bell-bottoms, fitted jersey cotton pants with matching collarless jackets, scandalously short mini-skirts and sheath dresses, and short-shorts for dressy attire, not only for casual and beachwear. All were styles that she would never have dreamed of wearing herself, but she was willing to experiment on me. It was the precursor of styles to come in the early '70s, when, for example, hot pants would come into vogue. I loved and hated it, all at the same time.

On a 1968 visit to Washington, D.C., with college roommate, Janice Booth, the author wears a navy blue wool crepe sleeveless sheath dress with white piping—still one of Sidonia's most popular styles.

"So, Hani, I hope you don't mind den I make dis skirt hem twenty-nine inches fun da floor," she said to me one day, staring up at me from the floor during a fitting, her yardstick in hand.

"Yes, Ma, I do mind," I responded, looking at the spot

where the yardstick had landed on my upper leg, barely covering my undergarments. "I don't think I can get away with wearing such a short skirt to class. Can't you at least go down one or two inches?"

"No, Hani, dat is not possible. You gonna have to vear it dis vay. Your legs are just right for dis lent," she said, never having learned to move her tongue forward to her upper teeth to form the "th" sound. "I can't change it. Anyvay, *tzi nisht azoy geferlekh*." There was that Yiddish line again, telling me it was not so terrible.

"Okay, Ma, if you say so," I replied, with a combination of reluctance and admiration for the extraordinary beauty of the garment on my body.

I finished the requirements for my Master of Arts degree in a little more than a year and a half. Conveniently, during the last few months of my graduate program, I had slipped in an independent study module on American history, partially satisfying my interest in history, which I had not pursued during my undergraduate years due to my lack of confidence in my own decision-making. It was also during that first lonely year of graduate school, when I remained at home, that I rekindled my friendship with a young man from Connecticut with whom I had spent time during my high school and undergraduate summers, and who was the only one who had accompanied my mother to my college graduation.

Likewise, in my imagination, Sidonia was also thinking of a young man.

When she was ready, Sidonia told her sister all about the young man with whom she had been keeping company. She relayed how comfortable she was with him, as he had gone through similar experiences during the Holocaust. She told Laura that this could be the person with whom she wanted to spend the rest of her life. Although she knew Samuel was younger than she was, she still did not know the real age gap that existed between them, perhaps afraid to ask for fear of learning the answer.

Laura was surprised by her sister's pronouncement and concerned about Sidonia after hearing her gush about the young man. Normally a sober, sensible, and cautious young woman, Sidonia was not usually so quick to form an opinion about someone, especially a man about whom she actually knew very little. Yes, they had just been through an extraordinarily painful period in their lives, Laura thought, and she had observed that many survivors at the camp had married quickly in an effort to compensate for their suffering and losses. But her sister seemed to be rushing into a relationship without giving it the deliberation she usually brought to bear.

Laura still spent many hours in her bed, sleeping much of the day, and barely eating her meals. After her liberation, her heart remained severely weakened as a result of the hard labor and the ravages of typhus. Yet making sure her sister was safe and secure, and not led astray by someone who did not have her welfare in mind, was most important. Laura was sure Sidonia would survive, although she, herself, might not. If Sidonia were to be the only remnant of the Perlstein family, she would have to make decisions that would restore her life and assure a successful future.

Sidonia's sister was interested in meeting this man, but first she wanted to ask someone at the DP camp what they thought of him. How serious was Samuel about a commitment to her sister? There was one person who would have all the information she was seeking and would be willing to provide it: their roommate, Simcsu.

Like Sidonia, Laura could appear nonchalant and unemotional when listening to stories relayed by other people—even those that were riveting and exposed sensational bits of information. While *not revealing her reaction, Laura learned some startling facts from Simcsu about Sidonia's lover.*

The truth was devastating. Not only was Samuel very young, barely nineteen years old, but he had never been in a relationship before and had no intention of developing a long-term liaison. His surviving family, Simcsu heard, had been fervently trying to dissuade him from continuing the affair with an older woman, although they did not know Sidonia's actual age.

Based on the information she learned, Laura felt that her sister should probably end the relationship as soon as possible. But how should she tell Sidonia? True to her wise and judicious nature, Laura waited until she actually met Samuel to make her final assessment. Laura began to prepare for the meeting with the man about whom she had already learned so much.

The meeting took place in the room occupied by the sisters and Simcsu, where Laura could remain close to her bed. The man, Mr. Yungman, came into the small room with Sidonia, holding a black beret in his hand, wearing a dark blue wool pea coat and black pants, and sporting a slick pompadour hairstyle piled high on his head. He was a tall, gangly, youthfully handsome man who seemed a bit nervous but wore a constant wide smile. Laura asked him questions about himself, wearing the same face she had displayed when she heard the details about him from Simcsu—nonchalant and unemotional.

A Hungarian-speaking Romanian, he told her that he had come from a large family, some of whom had perished in the Holocaust; those who had survived lived in various displaced persons camps. His closest brother in age had joined him there at Bergen Belsen. He explained that he did not have much formal education, but he hoped some day to go to university and experience life as much as possible. When Laura asked him how he felt about her sister, his response was much less specific. He had enjoyed meeting Sidonia and getting to know her, he replied, but time would tell what was in store for his near future. He did not reveal any real feelings for her sister nor mention any plans for a life together with her.

Later that evening, in their native Hungarian tongue, Laura told Sidonia her perspective on the young man, saying, "Sidi (Sidonia's nickname), he seems to be a little shy, but at the same time, he is also a bit cocky," she said, speaking softly. "He's very much a typical teenager. He is handsome and charming. I can see how you would like him. But he is naive about what it takes to make a committed relationship."

"But I know he cares about me. He is so gentle and understanding. I've never known anyone like him," Sidonia retorted.

"I understand. But Sidi, you are much older than him. I know this is hard to hear, but he's not ready to behave like an adult," Laura explained. "When the right time comes and we are able to leave this place, you could find a more mature man, closer to your own age, someone who could make good decisions about a life together. This young man is just not in a position to do that. I'm so sorry, but that's my view."

Sidonia could not say anything. She respected her sister's opinion and realized she was right about it all. It was a sober and frank evaluation about the man that she had hoped would be her partner for the rest of her life. She had been so enamored with Samuel that she had ignored all the warning signs. Amid her tears, she admitted to her sister that things had gone farther than Laura had thought. She was pregnant.

For quite some time, not recognizing the physical signs, Sidonia had not realized she was pregnant. During her time in the camps, she had not menstruated. The stress and physical toll on her body had abruptly interrupted her menstrual cycle during the year she spent in the ghetto and the three concentration camps. Barely feeling human, she had not thought about her womanhood during that horrible time. Even after a year in the displaced persons camp, she had just recently begun her regular cycle again and had not given a thought to a possible pregnancy.

Sidonia considered her next steps. She trusted her sister and appreciated her frankness. She chided herself for not thinking clearly about her entanglement with such a young boy. How could she have let this happen? If not for Laura, Sidonia might never have been able to think clearly about how to address her challenging circumstances. Now she knew what she had to do: end the relationship with Samuel. But then, what about the baby in her womb?

The question was answered for her only two days after revealing her situation to her sister, Waking up in a pool of blood and cramping heavily, Sidonia immediately knew that she was experiencing a miscarriage. Looking at Laura, sleeping in the nearby bed, she wondered whether she should wake her up. At the same time, Laura opened her eyes to see that Sidonia was in distress and recognized the reason for her pain.

"Sidi," she said, with tears in her eyes, "do you want to go to the camp hospital? I think I am well enough to go with you."

But Sidonia did not want to go to the hospital. "No, Lori, no. Let me just stay here and see it through. Don't worry. I'll just wash up and try to rest for a while."

Newly married couples, having wed quickly after their freedom at the camp, went to have their babies at Glyn Hughes Hospital, the camp medical center named after the deputy medical director of the British Second Army, who led the relief efforts during liberation. Survivors were giving birth at a rate deemed highest in the world at the time. But Sidonia could not stand the thought of facing all the couples that happily waited for their baby's arrival, a symbol of renewal and rebuilding of their lives. In her usual stubborn manner, *she vowed to treat herself without a doctor's care. She rested for a few days, while Simcsu brought her meals and aspirin, and eventually regained her strength and spirits. Laura was pleased that her sister had recovered so well, but also relieved that she would not bear the burden of a child in a very uncertain future.*

Sidonia never told Samuel about her pregnancy or miscarriage. Her sister had helped her realize how mistaken she had been to enter into a relationship with someone who lacked the maturity to act as a committed partner. Refusing all his advances to see her again, she observed that he soon ceased his attempts. Crying herself to sleep every night, she tried to reassure herself that she had made the right decision to not rekindle the relationship. She felt fortunate that her sister Laura was there to console and advise her.

Unfortunately, Laura's health continued to deteriorate. She became so weak that she was unable to rise up from her bed. After she was taken to the camp hospital, she lingered there for a few more days, but nothing could be done to improve her poor physical state. Sidonia's prayers for her sister's recovery this time were in vain. Laura died with Sidonia at her bedside on Friday, August 29, 1947.

Laura was the "somebody" that Sidonia needed to give her familial advice and emotional support. When everyone else had been taken from them, they had relied on each other to navigate through the struggles they faced after the most gut-wrenching experience they could imagine. Sidonia was not sure she could go on living without her sister. Still, she remembered that before her death, Laura had spoken seriously to her.

> *"Sidi, I love you so very much," Laura had told her. "No matter what happens to me, you must push on and live your life. Don't let anything stand in your way. You need to be the strong survivor of our beloved family."*

Those words would remain in her heart and mind for the rest of her life.

CHAPTER 14

Directional Stitching

> Most of the seams you stitch are neither straight-grain nor true bias. In other words, most seams are "off-grain." In loose-weave fashions particularly, such seams are easily pulled out of shape. In order to guard against this, it is good to acquire the habit of stitching *directionally,* i.e., *with* the grain and not against it.
> —"Machine-Stitching," page 118

My male friend from Connecticut happened to be in a romance with one of my high school classmates during that last summer of my graduate school studies. Although he seemed enchanted by her, the relationship concluded by the end of the summer. We began to date that fall, when I took a job in Connecticut as a seventh grade social studies teacher, still not knowing where my professional life was ultimately headed. I moved out of my mother's home and shared an apartment with a roommate in Connecticut to be closer to my work.

I was quite popular with the seventh grade students, likely due less to my expertise as an educator and more to two other factors. First, I was not much of a disciplinarian—similar in that way to my mother—but lacking the same tacit moves she used to successfully control my behavior. Second, my fashion style may have left a distinct imprint on my students. My mother, true to form, tried to clothe me in the modern styles she thought would be appropriate for my situation at the time. Just as she had designed casual clothing for a college student and business attire for my summer job at G. Fox & Company, she now created teacher's clothing for my job as a twenty-two-year-old educator.

However, what most educators would think was appropriate clothing for a teacher was not the same attire that my mother envisioned. She created mod, avant-garde designs in bold colors and mini lengths, using exclusive fabrics, like silk-satin. At times, my long, exposed legs seemed to leave very little to the imagination. The designs were beautiful and fit me like a glove, but were quite overwhelming for seventh-graders and my teaching colleagues. Although I had begun earning money of my own, I still wore my mother's homemade fashions rather than purchasing apparel at retail stores. I guess I did not want to disappoint her, and well, wearing her creations had become a way of life.

The seventh grade boys gawked at me; the seventh grade girls envied me; and my colleagues most likely were stupefied. One day, the principal, appalled by my raspberry micro mini-dress, chastised me for acting as a terrible role model for my students. I never told my mother that my boss had derided my choices in clothing, but the next time I came home to her, I took a more diplomatic tone than I had in the past:

> "Ma, how about making me a professional-looking suit with a longer skirt and jacket for work? I think that would be perfect."
>
> "Hani, no vay. I not gonna make someting dat is too old for you. You a young girl. You need clothes dat oder kits your age are vearing," she insisted.
>
> "I know, Ma, and I like those clothes, but maybe mixing it up with some more mature things might do me good at my teaching job."
>
> "Vell, I gonna do my best, but I don't tink it's a good idea," she chided.
>
> "I hope you'll think about it, Ma."

This kind of debate was one I never could win. She never changed my clothing style. I continued to wear the chic, often misplaced clothes she created and did so for a long time. As I reviewed my students' written end-of-year evaluations, I gleaned that my mother's style choices may not have been as misguided as I thought, after all.

> *... It seemed every 6th period, I met you on the top floor ... I was looking at those legs that turned out to be my teacher's. I think more teachers should dress and be as hip as you ...*
>
> *... You got a real good figure and nice legs. Your clothes are always neat and pretty ...*
>
> *... Good thing for the boys: You are pretty and wore short skirts ...*
>
> *... You dressed pretty good all year and that has an effect on the way you teach ...*
>
> *... So what's a nice teacher like you doing in a school like this?*
>
> *... I love you ...*

> Dear Mrs. Honey Marcus
>   I love the way you do things and I'm sure your husband does to.
>   Love always and a half
>   Mr. Handsome boy

An example of a student critique

CHAPTER 15

Pressure on Presser Foot

> Pressure on presser foot is regulated by pressure regulator, which may be a thumbscrew on top of machine or a dial inside. Locate it on your machine. Amount of pressure needed varies with weight, finish, fiber, and bulk of fabric. When pressure is correct, the two pieces of fabric—top and bottom—are held firmly but lightly in place and the two travel under needle at the same rate.
> — "Machine-Stitching," page 115

In reality, Sidonia gave birth to a baby girl in 1947 and managed to continue on her own at the displaced persons camp until June 1949. She never saw Samuel again nor did she spend time with any other man during that period. She bought a used Köhler, a 1920s German-crafted console sewing machine, and provided sewing services for others in the camp in order to purchase items such as dishes, Sabbath candelabra, down blankets, and clothing. She became a somber introvert over those years and decided to immigrate to the United States as soon as visas became available. Neither going back to the country that had helped to destroy her family nor immigrating to anywhere else seemed to make sense to her.

After a few weeks at Camp Wentorf in northern Germany, near the port city of Bremerhaven, she and I processed our immigration papers, fulfilled medical requirements, and set sail on the USAT *R. L. Howze* at the end of June, arriving at the port of New York on July 3, 1949, with only a few dollars in Sidonia's pocket. Her visa document indicated that she would become a seamstress to prevent her from becoming a public charge in the United States. Just a few days later, we arrived by train in Springfield, Massachusetts, our eventual American home.

Another pose for Sidonia's visa photo, previously unseen

The Springfield Committee for New Americans arranged for us to rent a room in the home of someone active in the Jewish community, someone who had taken in refugees in the past. Sarah Alpert gave us a room in her stately Victorian multi-family home in the city's North End in exchange for Sidonia's sewing and ironing services for her and her two adult sons, Gerald and Arnold. Sidonia grew to admire and respect Mrs. Alpert, an immigrant herself.

After a couple of years of citizenship class, Sidonia quickly learned to speak English and was ready to take on an American job. Using Mrs. Alpert as a reference, she secured a job at the Victoria Dress Corporation in the South End as a sewing machine operator. Charles Podell, the company's owner, was dumbstruck by her speed and accuracy at the machine, noting that few in the dress manufacturing business could equal her talent. He began to give Sidonia some special assignments, and in a while, promoted her to forewoman, a job that placed her in contact with managers and administrators in the garment industry.

In my imagination, this exposure to executives in the garment world allowed my mother to meet the man who, in my mind, would be the love of her life.

Sidonia met Henry at a meeting of garment industry business executives, where Mr. Podell had asked her to join him. He was a tall, pipe-smoking, no-nonsense, yet jocular man of forty, the same age as Sidonia. He had been married before, but his wife had died of cancer as a young woman and they had never had children. He was not looking for a new woman in his life, but something about Sidonia intrigued him.

She was not like most of the women Henry knew. Her air of confidence, cleverness, and her rising reputation in the garment business drew Henry's attention. He wanted to ask her to dinner, but Sidonia gave him the impression that she was not interested in men, either because she was too shy or perhaps her recent experience in the Holocaust as the sole survivor of her family, of which Henry was aware, had made her wary of relationships. Yet, he felt he had to take the chance.

Henry had analyzed Sidonia correctly. Although exhibiting an aura of confidence, Sidonia was also shy regarding men, having had no romantic relationships in her life beyond the deflating one with Samuel. She was not sure how to act around men, particularly Henry, whom she found extremely attractive. When Henry asked her to dinner after their first meeting, Sidonia's instinct was to say no, but almost against her will, she found herself accepting the invitation.

Henry and Sidonia found they had much in common, including their age, their Jewish faith, their interest in creative design, textile, fashion, and their mutual enthusiasm and ambition to succeed in the garment business. They continued to keep company, going to quiet dinners, attending the theater, and taking in movies.

Sidonia understood that this relationship was much different than the one she had been in at the displaced persons camp. It was 1953 then, eight years after her liberation at the end of World War II. She daily yearned for her lost family, especially Laura, but she had learned to live on her own, make a living, and fend for herself. She remembered Laura's words just before her death, "push on and live your life, no matter what ... be the strong, resilient survivor of the family." Desperate for the affection that Samuel had provided her when they were displaced persons, she had ignored his chronological and emotional immaturity. Now, she was profoundly changed. Henry's character, wisdom, and experience were what she needed.

After six months, Sidonia felt comfortable telling Henry about her failed relationship soon after the war, confessing that it was a confusing chapter in her life that she had stowed in her past. Henry, in turn, confided that while he had enjoyed a more positive relationship in his marriage, he had experienced a deep depression after his wife's death. He was not seeking a woman to take his wife's place, he explained, but he had fallen in love with Sidonia and hoped that she felt the same. When she acknowledged the same feelings for him, he asked for her hand in marriage. Finally, Sidonia had found someone with whom to forge a life, someone who would prevent her from living in total loneliness. If only Laura were alive to share in her happiness! She replied "yes."

They were married in 1954 at Mrs. Alpert's home, with a rabbi officiating and Sarah and her two sons acting as witnesses. The wedding took place soon after Sidonia became a naturalized citizen of the United States. Thanking Sarah Alpert and her family for all of their kindness, Sidonia left the Alpert's home as she and Henry moved into a newly purchased 1920s-era Cape Cod house in the Forest Park neighborhood of Springfield.

Sidonia bore a son, David, during that first year and decided to become a stay-at-home mother, at least for David's first few years. Shortly after, with Sidonia's enthusiastic support and collaboration,

Henry opened a women's clothing store in downtown Springfield, named Sid's Place. The store featured women's relaxed leisure garments, like cotton and wool pants with matching tunics and shirts, jumpsuits, soft wool sweaters, including cardigans and pullovers, with matching-color skirts and capri pants, and relaxed cotton shirts and dresses. The fashions were an early forerunner of the casual culture that would overtake the country by the 1960s. As Sidonia was never fond of synthetic fabrics, she convinced Henry to stock mainly clothing in her favorite natural fabrics, such as wool, linen, and cotton.

Occasionally, when she had the time, she would create a design of her own on her home sewing machine in a few sizes and Henry would sell it at the store. Sidonia's special designs became quite popular and demand for them increased rapidly. However, she was content staying home with her son and had no desire to expand her creative production. Four or five designs each year was enough to satisfy her creative urges.

Within another year, at the age of forty-two, Sidonia bore a second son, Martin, and decided to continue staying at home, becoming a real baleboste, *a true housewife who excelled at managing her home and family. Meanwhile, Sid's Place enjoyed steady business with many faithful customers, keeping Henry and Sidonia's family in comfort. They bought a bigger home in the nearby suburb of Longmeadow and became important members of the community. After residing there for a couple of years, Henry won election to the Town's Planning Board and assisted in the development decisions for the future of the community. Life was good.*

CHAPTER 16

Fitting a Garment

> Fitting a garment while sewing it should be a very small operation, involving small changes, the real alterations (if any) having been made in the pattern. If you want to check certain points in your garment ... you can try on the section in question as soon as the requisite darts and seams are stitched ... As a rule, however, fitting is done when all seams are stitched except side seams, waistline, and armhole seams, which should be basted. This will give you the total picture. Have someone help you. An adjustment is awfully hard to make on yourself ... do not fall into the error so often made by amateur dressmakers: *Do not overfit!* — "Fitting a Garment," page 89

When I was younger I never dreamed of a fancy wedding, an idyllic honeymoon, a dazzling diamond ring, or the details of my wedding gown. As a matter of fact, I never even thought about someday having a husband or children. I had learned about other girls' dreams at UMass, when some of the students in my dormitory talked of their fantasies of a beautiful wedding, marriage, and babies. At the time I thought, *What are they talking about? Is this what girls have on their minds?* I could not identify with their dreams.

I was not averse to the thought of marriage and children. It just never entered my mind as something upon which to pin my hopes. As a child and adolescent, my thoughts centered on finding a husband for my mother and a father figure for me, and most of all, sparing my mother from further pain or suffering, all while taking seriously my job as her fashion model.

I never really understood the whole dynamic of the relationship between the sexes. Although I only observed it as an outsider, never having viewed it up close in my own household, the concept seemed to involve deference of the wife to her husband. As I looked at the marriages around me, and those I viewed on American television, I noted that the man's wishes seemed to be predominant over those of the woman, a phenomenon that was totally foreign to me. No matter how strange it seemed, I simply assumed that marriage must be based on that paradigm and I would have to conform to it, whenever I entered into the institution.

Nonetheless, later in the winter of that teaching year, and after only a two-month engagement, I married the man who had been my friend for so long. Unprepared as I was at the age of twenty-two, I had developed a deep affection for him and felt he would make a good marriage partner. Although I was at a disadvantage on the subject of marriage and relationships, I thought it was time I attempted to develop my own identity, apart from the pressure of my mother's desires.

Marriage fit right in with my mother's plans for me. She hoped that it would mean that society would accept me, a woman with a husband and eventually children, a status she felt she had never been able to achieve. Again, she did not need to voice her wishes since I seemed to obey them, anyway. In her mind, he might also have fulfilled the ideal of a male role in our family, something we had been missing.

The nuptials took place on the snowiest day of the year at the very end of December 1969. Guests, including bridesmaids, were immobilized in blizzard conditions at airports and train stations and some never made it to the ceremony. Planned as a small wedding, with no music other than the Hebrew folk music sung by the officiating rabbi and cantor, it was a quiet, serene occasion attended by a group of close friends. My simple homemade wedding dress, of course, was stunning in white peau de soie.

"Han (yet another variation of my name), you making a good decision. I love him already like a son. You gonna be very happy," my mother confided after the reception on that cold December wedding day.

"I hope so, Ma," I responded, already wearing my parting ensemble, a white wool sleeveless sheath dress with matching coat.

"You gonna see. You gonna be a real *baleboste*," she said, while looking beyond my face as though already envisioning me with my apron around my waist and baby in my arms.

The parting wedding ensemble. An ivory sleeveless wool sheath dress with matching full-length coat.

I faltered at my initial attempt to satisfy my mother's desire for her daughter's perfect wedded bliss. The marriage was difficult from the very start, marked by childish, petty arguments over things I cannot even recall. My mother visited us that first week after the wedding since we could not afford to take a honeymoon and had to remain home in our tiny new apartment. As she viewed the spats we could not resist initiating, even in her presence, she could have intervened and suggested a time out between us or whisked me away to her house for a day. She did not do so. Looking back, I believe she wanted my marriage to work so much, possibly too much, in order to assure that my life would be better than hers. She decided to leave us, hoping that we would work things out as a couple without her intervention.

"Hani, I know your marriage is hard. But you just have to get used to each oder. Dat's all. You can do it," she advised me a week later.

"I'll try, Ma. I do care for him and want the marriage to work out. I really do.

"Hani, believe me, you can do it. Bot of you need to bend a little. It vill vork out okay. You vill see," she said, as though she was attempting to convince herself that all would be fine.

We worked it out to a certain extent and remained married, moving to a bigger apartment in Manchester, Connecticut, in 1971, when I left my short teaching career and finally decided to put my degrees into practice. Maybe there was hope for my marriage and a clearer view of my professional future in store after all.

In the spring of 1971, at the age of twenty-three, I made the decision that proved to be crucial in promoting my own positive self-image—and one not overshadowed by my mother's desires. I began to work as a social worker for the City of Hartford at a field office called Northside, deep in the city's North End. Arriving just a few short years after the riots following Martin Luther King

Jr.'s assassination, I found myself in a small two-story building with barred windows that housed workers from the city's health department, visiting nurses, a school busing program, state social workers, and our enclave of city social workers operating a local welfare program. All of us worked in minimally furnished partitioned offices that lacked doors and privacy. Surrounding us was a neighborhood rife with unemployment, addiction, poverty, and most of all, despair.

After my first few weeks of anxiety about working so close together with others and interacting with clients who lived in such challenging life circumstances, I found my footing. I discovered that acting as a catalyst for change on behalf of my clients and empowering them to overcome the systemic barriers they faced was as rewarding an experience as I had ever had. This was the way I could best use my psychology and counseling degrees, and at the same time, contribute to my family's economic security.

I was good at what I was doing and felt fulfilled when I returned home every day to my marriage, strained though it was. Through this job, I gained the confidence to finally crystallize my vision of my professional future, a task I had yet been unable to accomplish. It was the beginning of my self-verification.

Working as part of a team, a phenomenon that I had never fully experienced before, except to a limited degree during my summer at G. Fox & Co. and in my short teaching career, was a revelation. The free exchange of ideas and perspectives with my work cohorts, who ranged from social workers and educators to nurses and environmental health inspectors, not only broadened my knowledge base, but also made me feel part of a cohesive unit. All of us worked together in that small fortress in a neighborhood that not long before had been teeming with violence and unrest and had yet to fully recover. Still, we felt safe and secure with one another and formed friendships that would last a lifetime.

At times, sobering events occurred that tested our cohesiveness at the Northside office. When Ann, a young State of Connecticut social worker at our office, was accidentally stabbed while attempting to deflect a struggle between a client and his girlfriend, her death caused a time of deep sadness and reflection for all of us social workers. Her unfortunate killing made me seriously rethink my commitment to my new profession and whether I was willing to risk harm to work in such challenging circumstances. It was a question that all of us asked ourselves. However, in short order, I confirmed to myself that it was to be my life's work, despite the risks. Undeterred, we all remained at our posts at the Northside field office.

We often observed our clients incarcerated for crimes or devoured by the abyss of addiction or mental disorders. Poverty and unemployment were the most desperate human conditions that pervaded the community. Clients' deaths due to disease or violence, or the tragedy of a child's diagnosis with a grave medical condition, such as sickle cell anemia, also occurred with relative frequency. The seriousness of our work and our mutual trust served to bind my coworkers and me together.

My mother was proud that I had obtained a meaningful occupation. She proceeded to her sewing room and produced her usual high volume of what she deemed appropriate attire for a social worker. Meanwhile, I never revealed to her details about the vulnerable environment in which I worked.

During my work in Hartford, she may have reached the highest level of her fashion productivity of any time in her life. She thought nothing of it, but it was an era that I often referred to as "the marathon," because of its seemingly endless flow of fashions, one after the other.

Designs included the brown barleycorn wool tweed pantsuit and matching skirt, the multi-colored plaid Eisenhower jacket and matching bell bottom pants, the pink silk blouse with big tied bow, the peasant blouse and gypsy skirt with homemade suede belt, and the polyester print wide-legged pants and tunic top. Her productivity was so high that I was able to appear in a different outfit daily over a two-year span, which did not go unnoticed by colleagues and clients alike. The voluminous upscale fashions were so routine to me, I never noticed the disparity between my attire and the distressed environment in which I worked.

A barleycorn wool tweed pants suit

The author and Sidonia at a 1970s backyard gathering. The author wears polyester wide-leg pants with tunic top, diamond-shaped front bodice cut-out, and fringed belt. Sidonia wears black cotton pants and gray cotton tunic with red and black horizontal stripes.

Meanwhile, in my imaginings, Sid's Place grew into one of the most popular specialty stores in Springfield. Even girls and women from various surrounding areas, like Longmeadow, Holyoke, Chicopee, and Ludlow, were drawn to the cozy-casual garments featured at the store. Customers hoped that one of Sidonia's creations would be available when they visited, so they could boast that they had a coveted signature "Sidonia" piece. Representatives of the New York garment district came to town hoping to talk Sidonia into creating a fashion line all her own. She listened to the offers and talked it over with Henry, but in the end, she decided to stick with her occasional designs—only for their store.

By the time Sidonia and Henry reached the age of fifty, they were making a comfortable living and did not need to add any additional responsibilities or the extra resources that would come with creating a "Sidonia" line of fashions. Accepting the garment district offers would have meant working full time and that was not something she desired. Whatever ambition Sidonia had about advancing her own talent was overtaken by her commitments to her husband and two sons. She was content with her decision.

As much as she loved her family, she could never find the right time or courage to reveal her terrifying experiences during World War II. Those were events for which there was no one-word nomenclature for a long while. The term "Holocaust" did not come into usage until the late 1970s, finally giving the world a short, descriptive term for the genocide that occurred in the years before and during the war. How could she possibly describe the horrific events of the time that had destroyed her entire family, and forced her into carrying out hard labor in humiliating, harsh conditions, filled with starvation, disease, and death? And how could she describe her last family member, Laura's, death after having survived the brutal experiences of three concentration camps? Even she could not make sense of what she had been through during that devastating period of her life.

Sidonia could not talk of it to Henry or to David or Martin. She had to protect them from the pain that she had endured. All she could muster were a few references to her life and family at home in

Hungary and mentions of her deportation and names of the camps in which she was interned. They knew to ask no more of her. So Sidonia kept most of her Shoah (the Hebrew word for "catastrophe," but used to refer to the Holocaust) experiences tucked neatly inside a corner of her heart and memory for the rest of her life. Ironically, it took more courage for her to keep them inside than to unburden her soul and release the details to her loved ones.

CHAPTER 17

Assembling a Garment

> Assembling a garment should be a simple, efficient procedure based on intelligent organization of work. All instruction sheets (primers) accompanying patterns follow to some degree a system called unit construction, the purpose of which is to eliminate waste motion and unnecessary handling ... This is, however, the simplest and most streamlined way of assembling a garment ... Unit Construction II (sleeves sewn in before side seams are stitched) on children's ... clothes ... And remember that these picture stories just give you the "When to." For the "How to" of sewing your garment, continue to consult your primer. — "Assembling a Garment," page 15

I had my first child in 1974, a daughter, Brenda, named after the beautiful, modern but spoiled Jewish American character in Phillip Roth's *Goodbye, Columbus,* along with the Hebrew name, Basha, after my husband's late mother. Deeply connected to my job and needing the money, I worked at the Northside field office until the day before I delivered her. My family's financial needs meant that I would not be able to stay at home before or after Brenda's birth for very long. Six weeks later, I was back at work, leaving my baby with a caregiver who was a prominent member of the local La Leche League, an organization promoting the positive benefits of breastfeeding. She promised to care for her as though she were her own child.

In turn, I promised to return every evening with the breast milk I expressed each day, alongside my friend and colleague, Paula, who had given birth shortly before me. Paula and I had gained some notoriety during our pregnancies by bringing a successful Equal Employment Opportunity suit against the city, forcing them to allow usage of our accumulated sick and vacation time during maternity leave. Family leave was a benefit that was unheard of at the time. After returning to work, the two of us would speed up the stairs to the kitchen of our office building when no one else was there, to dispense and store our breast milk. We did not need any machines or pumps, just the old-fashioned manual system.

It was astounding how much Brenda resembled her father in the first few years of her life—albeit a much prettier and more feminine version. It must have been her eyebrows and the shape of her face that struck me as so similar to my husband's. Yet, she definitely had some of my physical traits: a glimmer of a pointed chin, high cheekbones, and a slim frame.

She also had a stubborn streak that was unmistakable even from birth, resembling one of my mother's distinct character features. At the sheer presence of the baby, my mother displayed one of the happiest and most serene faces I had ever seen on her.

"I tell everybody dat you had da baby, Hani," she told me the day after Brenda's birth. "I vent downstairs and tell da Stambovsky's dat it's a girl. Dey say, Mazel Tov! An den I tell da people at da grocery store."

"That's great, Ma. I don't think the people at the grocery store know who I am but it's a nice gesture," I responded, just content that my giving birth gave her such pleasure.

"Dey don't care. Dey happy for you anyvay! I tell some of my customers and some *grine* too. Everyvon is happy!"

An endearing letter arrived soon later from a member of *di grine*, who had moved to Israel. She was so fascinated by a wallet-size photograph of my new baby daughter that she wrote to me in her broken English:

> *Thanks ... for the little picture. I do kipped in my valled. I thing she is not only the best dressed girl in the State of Conn, she is the moust beautiful in Conn ... I am so happy I thing forsing me to go and see for myself her ... So how is your mother? Give her my best wishes ... I do know how she is feeling having such a beautiful Doll ... Good luck to her and all of you.*   —*Frania*

Sidonia and baby Brenda, 1974

Surprisingly, it only took me a little bit of time to adjust to the new addition to our family. I had never thought of a future with children earlier in my life. I had never even been around babies or small children before, so it was literally a matter of on the job training. Moreover, my husband's childhood had been marked with tragedy and dysfunction. Although our baby was a symbol of a possible brighter future for all of us, she did not bring us closer together. While we maintained affection for one another, my husband and I also miscommunicated and fell into perpetual conflict. My commitment to my satisfying job, combined with my misguided and unsuccessful mission to fulfill the marriage paradigm, as I understood it, led to an invariably tense home life.

He began to spend more time at his two-way radio communications business as I continued to work every weekday at my Hartford social work job and then came home to my homemaker chores and caring for my child. We retreated into our own cocoons. Even though the birth of a baby did not necessarily bring the marriage together, her soft skin and adorable smile warmed my heart like nothing else had in my life so far. Although I had never imagined having children, I found that learning how to be a mother, while challenging and frustrating at times, was the most important and fulfilling task I would ever undertake.

David and Martin attended the Lubavitcher Yeshiva School until sixth grade, since the community of Holocaust survivors felt comfortable sending their children there, hoping to maintain their Jewish heritage. David excelled in his Hebrew and secular studies, always at the top of his class. Martin, a year younger, had a bit more difficulty with his studies. His teachers felt that he did not take his schoolwork seriously enough and should spend more time on his homework. Even so, Martin, like his brother, became adept at Jewish literature, language, history, Torah studies, spirituality, and traditions, making their parents proud.

However, Sidonia's sons were not very interested in the garment business so beloved by their parents. They were content to wear tee shirts, jeans, pullover sweaters and well-worn sport jackets, when they needed to wear one at all. Despite Sidonia's efforts to persuade them to fit for a special homemade shirt, vest, or jacket, they consistently refused. They respected their mother for her creative talent, but picking fabric, patterns, and standing for fittings was anathema to both of them. They would rather spend time with friends, play pinball, or follow the progress of the Boston Red Sox during the baseball season, occasionally traveling to Fenway Park with their father to see a home game.

Although Martin initially did fairly well in his studies at the Yeshiva, he encountered more severe learning issues when he entered public school in seventh grade. His grades began to markedly decline and he insisted that although he was trying his best, he had difficulty reading his assignments. His mood was frustrated and irritable and he became somewhat withdrawn. His grades continued to be in the average range or slightly below, and his teachers insisted that Martin was just not focusing on his studies and that he could do better. Although Sidonia and Henry had many parent-teacher meetings to get to the bottom of Martin's learning problems, they were frustrated at the school system's lack of progress in identifying Martin's learning issue.

Finally, soon after Martin entered high school, he was tested for a learning disability that had garnered little attention up to that point. Martin was diagnosed with dyslexia shortly before the Christmas holidays. Upon his return to school after vacation, his teachers began using adaptive teaching techniques with him, which succeeded in enhancing his learning capacity over the next three years. By his senior year, he had improved but was still considerably behind his class in his academic studies.

Although Sidonia and Henry worked for many years to attain a positive school experience for Martin, they were spared the same frustration with their older son. David continued in public school and graduated from high school as the valedictorian of his class.

CHAPTER 18

Simulated Kick Pleat

> We are all familiar with the spectacle of a kick-pleat that has "tucked out." Or with a kick pleat that is bulky to sew or wear. These troubles can be avoided by making a pretend pleat—a slit with an underlay, the underlay being attached to the partial lining you will in any case put in back of your skirt to prevent its "sitting out." — "Pleats," page 152

In 1975, I discovered that my mother had lied about her age. Adopting an age six years younger than her real one, she had shared this fake information with everyone in America, including me, during her first twenty-six years in her adopted country. It was only when she turned sixty-two and became eligible for reduced Social Security benefits that she searched for her Hungarian birth certificate through our local Congressman's office to prove her true age. It was confirmed. She was born in 1913, not 1919.

At first I was angry at this subterfuge. As time went on, I became accustomed to the fact that my mother was six years older than I had thought. It did not occur to me that she would have more difficulty adjusting to her real age than I. She had used the fraudulent age for so long, dating back to the Holocaust when she had adjusted it several times to convince Nazi officials to keep her alive for another day, that she had grown to believe it. She preferred to view herself as the younger woman. Looking back, had I been in her shoes, I probably would have felt the same.

Sidonia's birth certificate from the county registry office in Hungary

When she turned seventy, according to her actual age, I innocently asked my sister-in-law to join me in taking my mother out for a celebratory lunch. As I proposed the luncheon to my mother on the phone, she seemed to accede to the idea of an event to celebrate her milestone birthday.

"Okay, Han," she said, "you sure you vant to do dis?"

"You mean take you out for lunch to celebrate your seventieth? Of course."

"Okay, den. I guess I gonna go, if dat is vhat you vant."

When feted at the restaurant by family and staff of the eatery, rather than smiling or acknowledging her happiness at reaching the age of seventy, she looked at me with daggers in her eyes and clenched her teeth during the entire meal, ignoring the food on her plate.

"Happy birthday, Ma. I'm so glad that we could spend this day together. Wow, seventy," I said.

She did not acknowledge my birthday wishes. She just squinted back at my face.

When we all loudly sang "Happy Birthday" to her, she tried to fake a smile, but it was a weak, puny one. I should have paid more attention to it. I must have thought that this was just part of my mother's serious nature. Wearing a somber face and not divulging much emotion was a way of life for her. However, this was something more. I realized only later that she resented the fact that I was emphasizing her real age since she, herself, had never totally accepted it. I was forcing her to not only confront it, but to publicize it. That must have intensely irritated her.

From then on, I did not focus on her real age very much, only when necessary, such as when giving information to her doctor or helping her renew her driver's license. She had no choice but to adhere to her new age, i.e., the true one, during the last thirty years of her life, but I knew it was not easy.

CHAPTER 19

Facings

> A facing is a piece of fabric that doubles and finishes an edge. It is usually a separate piece stitched to the edge ... but may be cut as an extension to the edge ... A facing is generally on the inside of a garment, but for a decorative purpose may be on the outside ... A well-applied facing has sharp, clean edges and smooth flat-lying surfaces. These are secured by attention to the small details in the application. ... Keep seam even; even a slight irregularity will show on finished edge. Use a seam gauge or mark seamline.
> — "Facings," pages 80 and 82

After working at the Northside field office for a few years, I encountered a snub, or at least a perceived rejection, that I had never shared with anyone. As part of the City of Hartford's police training, new officers were paired with social workers at our office to observe first-hand the kind of issues and problems our clients confronted in the neighborhood. To my surprise and dismay, I was not among the social workers chosen to perform this special tutoring module.

Was my supervisor sending me a signal that my job performance was not good enough to participate in training young police officers? My self-confidence was significantly tied up with my work. If that was not acceptable, then perhaps every other aspect of my life may have been unsatisfactory, as well. I could not face asking my supervisor why I had not been chosen and she avoided telling me, which I later realized was not an effective supervisory method. As I sobbed in my car on the way home from work that day, not sure why I was taking this supposed offense so seriously, I vowed to show my boss and my colleagues that I was worthy and more than capable of proficiently handling my caseload.

I never shared my professional disappointment with my husband or my mother, as I was not sure they would understand. It was my personal failure to own and rectify because it fed into that inferior sensibility of my dual unconscious. The impact of this professional slight mushroomed way out of proportion, and ultimately, motivated me to sharpen my social work skills and prove to myself that this was the work I was meant to accomplish. *I'll show them*, I thought to myself every day for a year.

> Just a couple months later, the supervisor approached me about managing a new caseload. "I've noticed that you have a special interest in our elderly and disabled clients," she said.
>
> "Yes, I enjoy working with that population group," I responded. "I guess I feel that they are the most at risk of all the clients we serve. They're fighting some courageous battles."
>
> "Then I think you might be the best caseworker here to handle our new SSI clients. From now on, I'll be assigning you those cases that are most likely to be eligible for the new federal program. You can walk them through the process and give them the professional support they need."
>
> "Thanks for the opportunity. I'll do my best," I responded with sincere eagerness.

Passed by Congress and approved by President Nixon in 1972, the Supplemental Security Income (SSI) program, operated by the Social Security Administration, offered federal support to low-income elderly and disabled children and adults. Memorizing all the

SSI rules and policies, I became the go-to person in the department for preparing individuals for their applications and appeals, if they were denied coverage. I knew the program backwards and forwards and could confidently face any administrative law judge when representing a client upon appeal. Over the following year, I built a fine reputation regarding client representation and public policy.

Letters I received from clients reinforced my confidence in my ability as a social worker and an effective representative of my clients' interests:

Dear Mrs. Marcus,

I am in the hospital looking for some alcohol answers. I will be out about the second week of January. My rent is paid to the first. I have been taken off all medication and want to make sure I will be ok without it. Maybe you could drop me a line. I would like to know about SSI. That first check would help a lot.

Best Regards,
Merle Garman

Or this letter from a client who secured work in another state and thought it was time he paid me back for my services:

Dear Mrs. Marcus,

I'm a long ways from you now and I miss you more than anyone else ... Think [sic] to you I do have a very good job and when I am back in Hartford I would like to stop in to say hello ... If you need any thing now all you have to do is let me know ... I would like to pay you back in any way ...

From a friend,
Dexter Bale

Or this, written on a 2" x 3" piece of scrap paper, from a client who would have liked to be my friend, but it did not work out:

Dear Mrs. Marcus,

You told me that you could allow me an order for a coat and a pair of boots, so do that, and then I would like you to close my case completely ... Sorry for the trouble I put you through ... It was nice knowing you but too bad we couldn't be friends with each other.
Yours Thankfully,
Dionne Bellmore

Or this letter regarding a client's concern about a doctor's bill, a dilemma many of us have faced:

Mrs. Marcus,

This Bill was sent here because my name was all mix up. Please see if it all can be straighten out. I never seen that much money in my life.
Sign,
Agnes Atwood

And the numerous letters from prison from an overly articulate client who waxed philosophical:

Dear Mrs. Marcus,

I hope upon receiving this letter you have been allotted by life all or most things necessary in containing a serene frame of mind as well as rewarding health ... Since I have last written, I have really gotten deep within myself in an effort of forming some type of concrete foundation as to just what my conception of life and the living of it can consist of ... It seems but a game of chance that everyone plays where no one can win without tasting each ball ... I am ready to re-enter the free world ...
Your Captivated "Brother"
Ex-client,
Louis

Receiving these pieces of correspondence and interacting with my clients in person taught me to watch the boundaries between social worker and client and to be aware of the psychological phenomena of transference and countertransference, in which counselor and client may each be transferring emotional reactions from her life onto the other. Although sometimes it was difficult, since I was sincerely empathetic and in some ways could identify with my clients, I understood the necessity of maintaining a professional relationship between us. I also understood the concept of transference from my clients to me, as evidenced by their letters. As their social worker, though, I prided myself on viewing them as individuals with growth potential even within their socioeconomic setting, and with my help in navigating the bureaucracies of the world around them, they could improve their lives the most.

A year after my perceived snub at work, as I had hoped, I was chosen as one of the social workers to mentor new Hartford police officers. Mission accomplished. Moreover, I had so impressed my supervisors that they offered me the opportunity to enroll in a Master of Social Work program at the city's expense if I promised to remain with the department for another two years. It was an offer I could not refuse. My husband helped me care for my baby daughter as I immersed myself in my studies back at the University of Connecticut. My mother was in favor of the decision to extend my education. If staying home with my family to become a real *baleboste* was not possible, then attaining more education was the next best thing to her.

"Hani, I hope you can do all dese tings, take care of your family and go to school at da same time. I know it vill be hard."

"I agree, Ma, I have to take advantage of this opportunity. It means I'll have the degree to advance my career in the social work field and financially help the family."

"You right. You doing da right ting, Hani. I understand."

With my mother's blessing and a clearer-than-ever view of my professional future, I felt confident returning to school to attain my second master's degree. By the summer of 1978, I had finished my degree credits, all the while continuing to work at my job. My published master's thesis was aptly titled *Supplemental Security Income: A Study of the Disability Determination Process*. I looked forward to what the city had in store for me over the next two years.

The masters thesis

Upon my degree completion, Hartford promoted me to the position of coordinator of a neighborhood service project in a different part of the city, and a year later, promoted me again to City Hall to supervise the managers of all the city's neighborhood service centers. My job satisfaction was the highest it had ever been and I was pleased with the promotions and the salary upgrades that came with it.

CHAPTER 20

Plackets

> A placket is a partial opening (i.e., closed at one or both ends) that allows a garment to be put in and taken off. It is more often in a seam, but may be cut at a slash in the fabric ... NOTE: Do not slash until you have reinforced point with stitching. If stitching line is not indicated on facing pattern, use a ruler to draw lines. — "Plackets," pages 146 and 148

The decision to have another child was challenging. My work was very important to me, both professionally and financially, and neither my husband nor I wanted me to quit my job. After a childhood and adolescence when I never envisioned myself with children, I was uncertain whether I wanted another. My tenuous marriage also made me think more than twice about introducing another child into our family. I finally came to the conclusion that Brenda should have a sibling to taunt, mentor, commiserate with, and share in the events of our household. My mother, thankfully, stayed quiet on the subject, although I am sure she desired another grandchild. Four years after having our first child, we finally decided to begin trying for a second.

It took more than a year, but we finally became pregnant and I gave birth to a son in 1980 named Stephen. My son's Hebrew name, Shimon, was derived from my maternal grandfather, the courageous man who had trained his daughters to be independent women. Almost two feet tall at birth, Stephen had a good head start on his eventual height of six feet six inches. His curly hair, like his sister's, long body, and piercing blue eyes, which would later change to brown, reawakened my maternal instincts and I began to yearn for another baby soon after his birth. The sober thought of my troubled marriage and job responsibilities brought me back to reality. I was back at work in a matter of a few weeks.

The author and baby Stephen

Although his lactation demands as a baby were daunting due to his large size, Steve was a relatively easy child to raise: not too whiny and as curious a child as ever was. Some of his earliest adventures included taking a phone apart in no time, darting off and wandering alone in shopping plazas behind our backs, and nabbing car keys from his distracted parents, all beginning at the age of two. I loved his precociousness but was also a little concerned that he was becoming a seasoned rascal at an early age. Even though he was named after my grandfather, he reminded me of the stories I had heard about my mother's brother, Dezso, the adventurer of his family before his brutal death in the Berga subcamp of Buchenwald.

Brenda and Steve

Stephen's birth set the stage for some changes in my work situation, which tested the bond with my mother that had been stable for a long time. By then, I was earning a decent salary, having been with Hartford for more than nine years and gaining another masters degree during my time there.

The schism occurred when Stephen was only five months old and Brenda was six. I decided to leave my job in Hartford for a new position as the human services director for the Town of Manchester, Connecticut, a medium-sized town just east of Hartford. I had applied for the new job in the summer of 1980 at a friend's urging after she saw the advertisement for the position in the newspaper. "Look at this job ad, Hanna," my friend said. "It's perfect for you! It almost has your name written on it."

Although I was not seeking a new employer, I was intrigued by its proximity to my home and interesting job specifications, combining coordination, networking, and supervision, all as essential tasks of the position. I interviewed for it late one afternoon, still wearing a nametag from a conference I had helped to sponsor earlier that day for my Hartford job. Just a few days later, I was excited to learn that the job was mine.

My mother thought my position in Hartford had been a terrific job with the kind of security and benefits she thought appropriate for her daughter. She was concerned that I was taking too much of a gamble by leaving a stable job for an uncertain one, risking job discontent, failure, or dismissal.

> I insisted. We had moved to our own home nearby in Vernon, Connecticut, only one town east of Manchester. "I have to do this, Ma," I said. "It's closer to my home and now that I have two kids, my presence could be needed more than ever. I'm willing to take the risk."
>
> "No, Hani, no," she pleaded. "You shouldn't leave a good

job mit good pay for von dat you don't know vhat could happen. Vhat if dey let you go and you don't have any vork?"

"It's worth taking the chance. It's about the same salary and closer to the kids' day care and school."

"You making a big mistake, Hani. I vish you vould tink about it."

"No, Ma. There's no thinking about this anymore. I'm doing it. I'm sure it's the right thing." I was surprised by the conviction in my voice when countering my mother.

She could not understand the rationale for taking risks, perhaps because she had been forced to take too many of them to survive the hardships and horrors of the Holocaust. Although she had told me of many events during that time, I always sensed that she had taken more risks than she had confided to me. And of course, there was the chance she took in conceiving a child with a young man who was unable to be a partner or parent.

I could not convince my mother that this decision was a good idea, and she was angry that I had taken such an important step without first consulting her. My husband supported the decision but my mother could not do the same. As I reflected on it, I understood that she viewed earning money as an indication of success in America, as evidenced by her frequent bank trips. Her motto had become: Don't take a risk when it comes to earning a living. Don't give up on a good thing.

Over the next few months, my mother called me less frequently and showed her hard feelings in her face and demeanor when we saw each other in person. When my mother exhibited her most dour face, she left a searing impression on me, one not easily forgotten. Our conversations were terse and greatly curtailed. I had followed her direction thus far in my life, so this was a distinct departure from my usual tacit acquiescence to her wishes. She was not accustomed to it.

I wondered if our relationship would ever be the same. We had kept much from each other during our life together, yet we had also always maintained a close bond, as long as I generally abided by her directives. It must have been hard for her to keep some emotional distance from me due to my job decision. I knew that it was difficult for me not to talk to her every evening and hear her supportive voice on the phone.

However, I think she slowly realized that the move was a good one. She began to understand all the advantages of my shorter commute and new job opportunities. Through her customer network, which by the 1980s reached as far as Connecticut, she also learned that my boss was a benevolent man, who had put me under his protective wing. The job was safer than she had originally projected. Within six long months, we returned to our regular mother-daughter rhythm.

Since I would be a department head, my job called for new, modern business attire. This development would usher in the fashion designs that would represent the height of her creative powers. It was her period of haute couture, meaning the highest level of design, tailored touches, and refinement she had ever endeavored to produce.

When I worked in Hartford, my mother's designs, although voluminous in number, fell into the business casual category. They were somewhat tailored but also trendy and often informal. Her designs for the Manchester job, which spanned more than twenty years, leapt to another level. She tuned in to the changing environment for working women, who began to make their mark in business, industry, and the public sector. The era called for an even more tailored look, marked by fully lined pants and straight skirt suits in bold fabrics and designs, some based on the classic works of designers like Chanel and Dior. Her suits became crisp and sharp, with well-defined, prominent shoulders and sleeves, and

A houndstooth wool and black felt suit

pleats of various sizes and shapes. Her fashions changed seamlessly with the times.

During the 1980s and 1990s, my mother's fashion output was as varied in fabric, style, features, and functions as it had ever been, yet it remained as haute as couture could be. As she aged from her late sixties to her late eighties, she continued to sew at a breakneck speed and her exquisite fashions dazzled all those who saw them. In the '80s, her designs included a black and white wool houndstooth jacket with standup collar and black skirt, a novelty weave gray wool pantsuit and skirt, a gabardine skirt and collarless jacket with contoured waist, a madras print and navy top with matching skirt and jacket, and many more.

A madras print set, including skirt, top, and jacket

A novelty-weave wool pants suit

Co-workers no longer needed to ask where I had purchased my ensemble of the day. After just a short while, they all realized that my mother created each and every one of my outfits.

"Hanna, your suit looks stunning today. Where did your mother get the idea for the design of that red and black wool suit?" a colleague asked.

"Well, I really don't know. She may have seen it in a magazine, or on television, or on a model or even in a store window. I really never know exactly how my mother gets her fashion ideas. She just surprises me," I responded.

"You're pretty lucky. I hope you have big closets!"

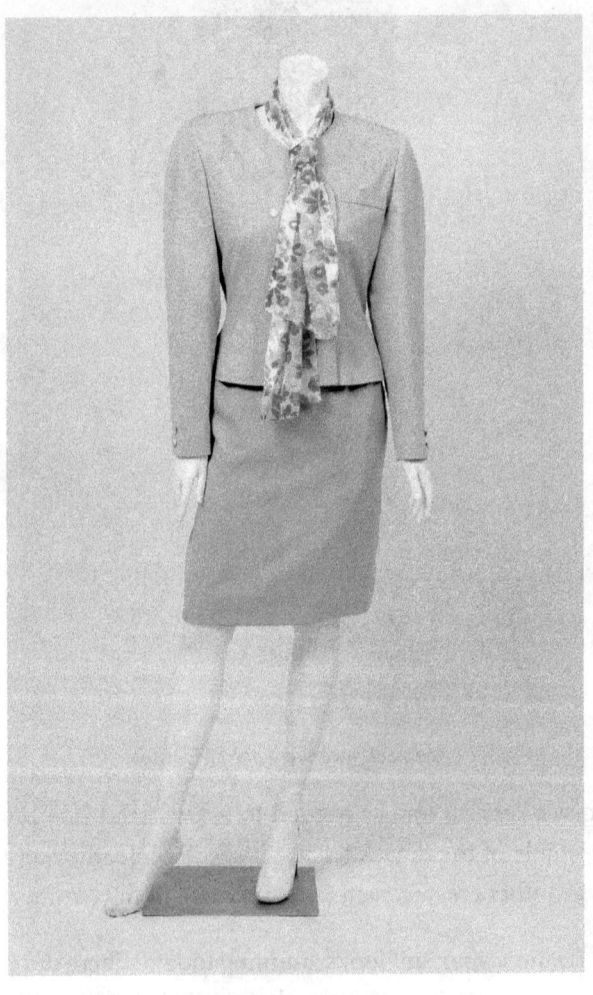

A light gray wool gabardine double-breasted suit with contoured waist and pearl buttons

I admired my mother's ability to dazzle me with her ideas. More often than not, without my input, she advised me of the next garment on her list of intended designs. Once she had the idea in her head and looked at a pattern, she could choose just the right fabric combinations and matching buttons to create a singular garment that would turn heads. She had a knack for finding comfortable yet fashionable designs that were ideal for my height and shape.

I was not fully aware that my couture, combined with my tall stature, might have afforded me an air of authority that gave my work an extra level of recognition. Although her creations may have been a bit too haute couture for a job setting in a working-class Connecticut town, they may ultimately have been to my professional benefit, just like my mini outfits of the late '60s and '70s, which had also brought me positive notice.

CHAPTER 21

Tailor's Tacks

> A slightly slow, but excellent method (of marking), suitable for all fabrics, leaving no permanent marks, and visible on both sides of fabric. Tailor tacks are made with needle and thread. Darning cotton and embroidery floss are best, because they stay in fabric better than other threads. Use a long thread, doubled, without a knot. At point to be marked, take a small stitch through pattern and both layers of fabric. Draw up, leaving a 1" end ... Cut thread, leaving a 1" end. Gently separate the layers of fabric ... and cut through threads. — "Marking," page 122

I always wanted to visit Hungary, my mother's birthplace and home until she was thirty-one. If I had viewed such a visit as sad or painful, I do not think I would have wanted to take the trip. Instead, the country and particularly my mother's village, Dámóc, always occupied a special happy place in my imagination. My mother's stories of her large nuclear and extended family, reaching back into the late eighteenth century, had comforted me when I had no other family except her in my real life. The characters and scenes in those tales induced my need to see the place where these joyful events occurred. I would not be deterred by the brutality and tragedy that eventually befell this family in that country.

We had not taken many vacations during my childhood, but it was easy to entice my mother to go on the trip in August 1983. We also took my nine-year-old daughter, Brenda, who at that early age assumed the role of trip photographer, a job she continued to maintain in our family. We planned to spend a week in Hungary and another week in London. Although I had never learned to speak much Hungarian, other than the days of the week, some numbers, and *hogy vagy* [how are you], I brushed up on some common Hungarian words and greetings before our trip and hoped I would have a chance to use them.

We stayed in Miskolc, Hungary's second largest city, with one of my mother's few living first cousins, Ferenc (Feri, for short), and his wife Sevi [pronounced "Shay-vi"]. They had returned to Hungary after World War II and the Holocaust and had built a family and a life there. Sevi had broken her leg before our arrival and was bed-ridden during our entire visit. She and her husband appeared content with their lives in a Soviet country. During our stay, Feri and his son, Laci [pronounced "Lut-si"], and his family took us sightseeing, including a stop for authentic goulash, Hungarian ice cream (more ice than cream), and a relaxing soak in the ancient thermal cave baths of Miskolctapolca [pronounced "Mish-koltz-to-pol-tsa"]. As I observed the Hungarian language spoken by her cousins and others we met in Hungary, I noted for the first time my mother's particularly melodious and precise spoken version of the language.

On one occasion, Feri responded to the doorbell and greeted a messenger, who counted out Feri's monthly pension in cash while standing in the doorway, an act that would never have occurred in my mother's adopted country. Upon the messenger's departure, Feri turned to my mother and said in Hungarian, "See, Sidike (an affectionate form of my mother's Hungarian name, sometimes just Sidi for short), we are not so suspicious of each other here like you Americans." To him, my mother was an American, no longer a Hungarian. She smiled and nodded, *"Igen, Feri, ez nagyon yó* [Yes, Feri, that's very good]."

The author and Sidonia at their cousins' home in Miskolc, Hungary, 1983. The author wears a polo shirt with one of Sidonia's print full-skirt designs.

Feri would act as our chauffeur to my mother's home village in the countryside the next day, a two-and-a-half-hour car drive. Since I have offered an account of my visit to Dámóc in a previous volume, I will not repeat it here. Suffice it to say, our day in the six-hundred-year-old village, noted for its predominantly Greek Orthodox Catholic community, was one of the most momentous days of my life. Seeing the bucolic hamlet on that steamy ninety-degree summer day, with its simple rustic houses surrounded by colorful flowers, rows of sunflowers, and plum and apple trees, brought my mother's tales of her happy, peaceful family life to reality. Moreover, its residents, who had been my mother's contemporaries as a child and young adult, fondly remembered her and members of her family by name, at one point lining the street with food and drink in celebration of her return. Their greeting confirmed that my mother had, indeed, been part of the fabric of a close-knit community. Her stories had been true.

This way to Dámóc

At the same time, noting that the residents who greeted us were mostly in my mother's age cohort, I wondered whether this tiny village would remain as vibrant as it had been in my mother's time and even on that very day we visited. As most of the villagers' offspring had departed the town to secure work in bigger cities, could this somewhat remote, inconspicuous hamlet exist in the future without its residents consistently working the land to continue their livelihoods?

The small amount of information I discovered on the internet about this miniscule location showed an increase in the number of residents in the last two decades, albeit still less than five hundred overall. Moreover, the data indicated that the median age by 2015 was in the forties, so the population was not elderly, as I had speculated. Could Dámóc have acquired some industry that boosted the town's economy and attracted younger residents? My curiosity about the town's current status gnawed at me. Knowing that the village must have endured a restructuring of land during the Soviet era and then transitioned again after Soviet domination concluded, I wondered about the implications of these changes on my mother's ancestral town—and what I would find if I ever returned, a trip I have yet to take.

On the day of my visit, I focused on viewing the village as it looked that day and imagining its existence in my mother's era. Observing my mother's childhood friends greeting her so warmly triggered the mixed emotions that I brought home with me to America. If the residents of her village cared for the Perlstein family so much, why did they betray them by allowing their deportation, even transporting them to the first way station on their trip to the ghetto in Ujhely? How did the transfer of the Perlsteins' property actually occur, including the house, its contents, the animals, and the never-found treasures hidden behind a stone in the kitchen? Despite a letter following our departure from the new owners of the home, attempting to assure us that they had no knowledge of the whereabouts of the Perlstein treasures, I felt that these

A villager hugs Sidonia upon her forty-year return to the town.

questions still remained unanswered. I swore to one day attempt to identify what actually occurred and perhaps hold some remnant of my ancestors' possessions in my hands.

Only after my return home did I concede that just as my ancestors did not fully realize the reality in store for them, the Greek Orthodox villagers also did not know. With only five Jewish families in the village, the gendarmes, who had given the deportation orders, would have known the names of all the Jewish residents and their locations. It would have been almost impossible to hide them. Even if the villagers could have somehow hidden the Jews, they would have been risking arrest, imprisonment, or death for themselves and their families. Undoubtedly though, observing the forced departure of their Jewish neighbors, the villagers must have known that their fate was dismal. Unlike my mother, who maintained warm feelings toward them, I still struggle after all these years to reconcile my conflicting views of my mother's former close friends and neighbors.

Before embarking on the next step of our journey, Budapest, we stopped in Sátoraljaújhely, the site of the Jewish ghetto in my mother's part of the country during World War II, where she and her family were interned prior to their departure for Auschwitz. At the time, I knew little about their experiences there since my mother only rarely spoke of it. She hoped that a surviving stepniece, Little Etel, who had written to her right after the war, might still reside there, but after searching and speaking to a couple of Jews who still remained, we concluded that she had probably left the city a long time ago. Fewer than ten Jewish families remained in Ujhely, not even enough to comprise the requisite number of participants for a religious service. The synagogue we observed as we traveled along the streets was shuttered.

"I so disappointed dat *Kis Etu* [Little Etel] is not here in Ujhely. I vould like to see her so much," my mother said dejectedly in the car, while clutching the watch she had brought as a gift if we had found her.

"I know, Ma. I guess it was pretty unrealistic of us to think she would still be in the same place after all these years. It looks like a lot has happened in this city since the war," I said, offering some consolation.

My knowledge of the details of my ancestors' stay and that of other Jews in the ghetto came only many years later, after my mother's death. Research using JewishGen, the Jewish genealogical online service, and the work of Meir Sas on the vanished Jewish communities in Hungary, detailed the characteristics, protocols, conditions, and timelines of the Ujhely ghetto. Those facts assisted me in imagining what the Perlstein family endured during the first step of their exile from their ancestral home. The gruesome conditions in the Ujhely ghetto assuredly set the stage for all the torturous events that occurred after their train ride from there to the death camps.

We spent our last two days in Hungary with cousin Feri's daughter, Eva, and her family in Budapest, a city so far from my mother's village in the northern corner of the country that the visit was a first for my mother, as well. We toured parts of the cities of Buda and Pest, wandered around Fisherman's Bastion, a lookout over the Danube River, and the Church of St. Stephen, the patron saint of Hungary. For some reason, perhaps due to their lapsed Jewish faith, our cousins never took us to the Dohány Street Synagogue, the largest in Europe, a visit I will make if I ever return to the country.

We ended our visit with a lunch in Eva's apartment. It was a dairy lunch featuring a delicious dish that I had never seen or eaten before, *szilvas gomboc* [pronounced "sil-vash gum-bots"], a traditional sweet plum pudding, made of potatoes, eggs, and sugar with a plum in the center.

I turned to my mother beside me at the dining table and asked, "Ma, how come I never had this dish before? Eva says everyone in Hungary eats it. Didn't you eat it when you lived here?"

"Vell, Hani, yeh, ve made *szilvas gomboc*. Ve had so many plum trees in our village. But I am too busy dese days to make such a ting. I never really feel like it," she replied apologetically.

"We should try to make it when we get home then, Ma," I said, with conviction.

"Yeh, maybe," she replied in a rather low tone.

Although my mother, too busy making a living and focusing on her sewing, was never known for her cooking ability, I was a bit taken aback by her almost total abandonment of the recipes with which she had grown up. Occasionally, she made a mean matzo ball soup (chicken soup with *knaidlach*) or noodle pudding (*lokshen kugel*), but I think these were recipes she learned from *di grine* after arriving in America and not from her life in Hungary. Even *goulash*, the beef stew dish so well known around the world, was a rarity in our household. Needless to say, we never made the *szilvas gomboc* upon our return home.

In many ways, our Hungarian trip showed me how markedly my mother's life had changed since she had forcibly left her home country and immigrated to America. Without her family surrounding her, and at the same time, facing the necessities of life as a single parent and immigrant, those homebred traditions had quickly eroded. The only tradition she had transferred from her ancestral to her adopted home was dressmaking.

Most importantly, our visit, more than any other event in my life, reminded me of the importance of time and place in each of our lives. When I observed my mother's home village in real time, I also viewed it as it might have been in my mother's world. As I spoke to the villagers that day, I imagined them as they might have been prior to the 1940s, enjoying the closeness and familiarity with one another and their communal way of life. Yet, I also sensed the silent undercurrent of bias that allowed the destruction of an entire family in their midst. Had I been born only one generation earlier, I understood that I would have lived among them and my ancestral family, who I never had the opportunity to know—and also, that I may have died an untimely and brutal death.

Only one generation had separated a life in a small agrarian village, etched by the horrors of the Holocaust, from a life lived in the comforts of a contemporary American existence. I realized that I had been, like all of us, placed on the earth at a particular point in the continuum of time that allowed me to encounter a vastly different place and set of circumstances. The full comprehension of the randomness of our individual emergence onto the time continuum was sobering and often daunting, but also enlightening. The timing and circumstances of my birth were conditions that I could not control. I could only imagine the past, and handed the circumstances of my birth, make the best of my present and future.

My mother and her cousin, Feri, and his wife, Sevi, corresponded for a while after our visit. Their letters proved to be very affectionate but also seemed to emphasize their misguided assumption that my mother had become an American and, therefore, was capable of granting favors to her more humble Hungarian cousins. Translated from the Hungarian, one letter read:

August 5, 1985
  Dear Szidike (retaining the "z" in my mother's affectionate name) és gyerekek [and children],
  We are truly happy when we receive a letter and especially such a nice letter as from you, Szidike. Thank you for the

photo that you sent. We were very glad to get it ... You really have a beautiful family and most likely happy. I know that it is so and that they are everything to you. That is why I want to doubly thank you that you are so good to my children. Laci came very excited to tell me that you will bring them for a visit to you. I would be very happy for it because he is very much longing for it ... no one has invited my children to visit which is something they very much wish ... Szidike, to this day, I am sorry that I happened to be sick when you were here. Everything is upside down in situations like that, but if you come again I promise you that we will make up for it ... Believe me Szidike, the only way we are able to live off the pension is if everyone is helping a bit. Write to me about everything, about the children ... I think we are not young anymore and it is good to meet often while we are alive.

We kiss everyone with a lot of love.

Sevi and Feri

As far as I knew, my mother and cousin Feri only met one more time, later in the 1980s, when he was visiting his niece's home in New Jersey. My mother, never very committed to correspondence, probably neglected to respond to future letters, and they ceased writing by the end of the 1980s. We never saw him, his wife, or family again.

Many years after our Hungarian trip, just a few years after my mother's death, I received a visit from Little Etel's son, who was just as eager as I to meet. We had found each other through research I had initiated through the International Tracing Service archives at the United States Holocaust Memorial Museum. I learned that his mother had come with her family to New York in the 1950s, after the Hungarian Revolution, and had lived in that state ever since.

She and my mother had, ironically, passed away at about the same time. He and I talked at length about our mothers' friendship and our sadness that, despite their proximity, they were unable to find one another during their lives in America.

We had searched for Little Etel in Ujhely, Hungary, yet she was so close to us all along. If only we had known during my mother's lifetime, we would have embraced a reunion with her step-niece, a namesake of her own sister, Etel. They had both gone to their deaths holding onto the memory of each other and their friendship together during happier times.

CHAPTER 22

Yardstick

> Indispensable for marking straight long lines, often used for marking hemlines from the floor. Should be firm and straight, with smooth edges and clear markings. — "Equipment," page 64

Actually, cousin Feri sent one more piece of correspondence when all the others had ceased. One day in 1988, we received a mysterious package from Feri and Sevi. When we ripped open the brown wrapping paper, we were surprised to uncover a poorly printed and bound paperback book, titled (when translated into English) *Dámóc: History and People,* published in Sátoraljaújhely, and issued by the Ujhely city council. The author was József Siska, a member of one of the families who were longtime residents of my mother's hometown. Feri must have thought my mother might be interested in this historical account of the town where she was born.

This one-of-a-kind book detailed stories of the residents and events of the village dating back six hundred years to 1364, when the village was named, up to 1987, the year of the book's publication. In addition to crudely drawn maps of an early Dámóc, illustrations of ancient coinage, photos and drawings of its residents' art and handiwork, and exterior photographs of the town's people and residences during the twentieth century, it also included letters and postcards from foreign lands, like America, or the home front during war times. Holding special interest for me, it also contained listings of names and occupations of every head of household at various intervals of time.

Written, of course, in Hungarian, the book seemed intimidating to me. I had the feeling that my mother may have glanced at the book's contents but never really read its narrative too closely. Ensconced in a drawer since its receipt, the book must have recently called out to me since I began to read as much as I could with my limited knowledge of the Hungarian language before I considered turning it over to a more qualified translator.

The earliest list of the town's residents that named ancestors of the Perlstein family was based on the 1869 Hungarian census and indicated the following:

One hundred and fourteen families lived in Dámóc at that time, including 428 children. Remarkably, the names of all 114 heads of household were listed, which included eight widows, along with their occupations. By far, the most common occupations were plot farmer and farmhand/day laborer. The exceptions to these usual jobs were clergyman/minister, chorus leader, notary, and blacksmith, all basic and necessary functions of a religious community, with occasional legal matters to address and the need to keep their horses shod and their metal tools crafted. The occupations of the few Jewish residents were more commercial in nature: David Perlstein, salt vendor; Marton Perlstein, general merchant; and Leopold Klein and Izsak Swartz, both tavern keepers.

In the 1870s and '80s, according to Siska, men from Dámóc began seeking more economic security for their families, and were drawn to cities in America and Canada. Although some may have remained in North America, many stayed for only a few years, sending money back to their wives and children. The book presented a long list of American cities and states where Dámóc residents settled, such as the states of New York, New Jersey, Pennsylvania, Wisconsin, and Ohio, and cities such as Pittsburgh,

Scranton, Youngstown, Trenton, Chicago, and Cleveland. After securing a nest egg in America, many returned to their family and Hungarian town to live out the rest of their lives.

Coincidentally, my grandfather, Simon, one of Marton's sons, also left Dámóc for New York City as a young man in the late nineteenth century, but stayed there less than a year, when homesickness and fears about dilution of his Jewish faith forced him to return. His departure for America may have coincided with that of his friend, Adolph Zukor, who decided to stay in America and eventually became a legend in Hollywood, thereby avoiding the tragedy that lay ahead for his fellow Jewish countrymen.

Later, in 1903, Marton Perlstein appeared again in a listing of townspeople in Siska's book. His occupation was still general merchant, but he had also added what appeared to be steam miller. This may have implied he was employed in the steam mills producing wheat flour, a popular industry in Hungary at the time, and involving an essential staple product such as bread. It could have been an occupation that was very advantageous to his community. I was unable, however, to discern his exact role in the flour mills, either as an owner, worker, or investor. In searching further, I could find no other Perlsteins listed on or later than this date.

The only other references to the Jews of Dámóc I could find in this book referred to the advent of Jewish merchants to the town in the early nineteenth century (hence, David and his lineage) and the permeation of Ruthenian and Jewish cuisine into Hungarian culture. In addition, the author mentioned the significant economic and human impact of World War II, when the village's Jewish families, who had played an important economic role in the small community, were deported in 1944. As I had seemed to reach the end of references to my ancestors, and after long contemplation, I decided not to enlist translation assistance for the rest of the book. I felt that I knew enough about many of my forebears through other well-documented sources, and had already learned some of their eventual sad fates as victims of the Shoah, which this book could not edify.

As I performed further research, with the assistance of JewishGen, I found that David Perlstein, my great-great-grandfather, was born in Dámóc in 1799, which implied that the Perlstein family probably had moved to the town at some time prior to his birth at the end of the eighteenth century. The JewishGen database indicated a sizable number of Perlsteins living in Hungary in the nineteenth century, with many located in Sátoraljaújhely, the nearest larger city. It was plausible that his family may have originally settled in that location and moved to nearby Dámóc before the turn of the nineteenth century, seeking a more agrarian way of life or, even more likely, an opportunity for business and trade. Starting with David, his descendants were loyal citizens of Dámóc for the next one and a half centuries. The names of his relatives and descendants were so numerous in the database that I was overwhelmed.

What's in a name? Everything. Names are not just meaningless labels of those who may have lived in the past. For someone bereft of family, like me, the names of my ancestors are a revelation. A name confirms that a person had existed in a time and place. It shows that my mother and I were not placed on the earth out of thin air. A family, whose members had certain characteristics, occupations, and traditions, had preceded us. The more names I uncovered, the more I felt that the people who were attached to them belonged to me and I belonged to them.

David married twice, first to Eszter, with whom he had two sons, Marton (sometimes referred to as Markusz or Mordkha), born in 1839, and Moritz, born in 1840. Another child, also named Eszter, born in 1846, appeared in some data as David's daughter, but her birth mother was not listed. After his wife Eszter's apparent death, he married Katalin, twenty years his junior, whose maiden surname was noted differently depending on the source. They appeared to have three more children, Ignacz (sometimes referred to as Izsak), Mitzi/Mali, and Mari. They and five of their children appeared as far back as the 1857 census.

David, Katalin, and their younger three children were counted again in the 1869 census, when David was seventy and still worked as a salt dealer, according to Siska's historical account, but he died in Dámóc in 1882. As a salt vendor and trader, he supplied the region with the precious mineral compound that preserved much of its nutrition, and was, therefore, one of the keys to its health and survival. Katalin, his much younger second wife, died before him in 1875.

A mystery surrounded Katalin's (sometimes referred to as Kati) faith, since the maiden names listed for her were Fisli or Gyergyamart, not traditionally Jewish names. It was possible that, like a number of other widowers with children in small villages, David was anxious to find a mother figure for his children and was willing to accept an arranged marriage with a young woman who may not have shared his faith.

His oldest son, Marton, my great-grandfather, also born in Dámóc, married Mali Grunfeld in Ujhely in 1862, and had at least seven children, Herman, Juli/Zali, Samuel, Simon, Hani, Lina, and Salamon, all born in Dámóc. Five of his children continued to live there even after their marriages. His children Simon, Samuel, Salamon, and perhaps Lina, and their spouses and children, were still residents at the time of their deportation in 1944, while other siblings had moved to nearby towns. They may have comprised four of the five Jewish families in the small village.

My grandfather Simon, one of Marton and Mali's middle children, was born in the town in 1869. Married to Hani Klein in 1895, he and his wife had six children, Szeren, Dezso, Margit,

Etel, Laura, and Sidonia (spelled Szidonia in Hungarian) all born in Dámóc. Margit passed away in 1918, taken as a teenager by the great Spanish flu pandemic.

Born during the era known as "the time of peace," which extended from the end of the nineteenth century until World War I, all of Simon and Hani's offspring were spared overt anti-Semitic acts and societal and educational restrictions for Jews during their early youth. However, by the end of World War I, the tide had turned against the Jewish population in Zemplén County and in the country as a whole. Anti-Semitic violence ensued and several Numerus Clausus laws were enacted during the 1920s, '30s, and early '40s, which increasingly limited Jewish entrance to universities, professions, and eventually business and home ownership and, in fact, all economic activity. The Perlstein family was forced to find creative ways to continue their livelihoods during a highly repressive time. As usual, they turned to commercial enterprises, such as trade, to informally continue their way of life.

Simon and Hani's only son, Dezso, an adventurer and rascal, was a veteran of the Hungarian army during World War I. His escapades involving newly illegal border crossings for contraband goods after the disintegration of the Austro-Hungarian Empire put him in the crosshairs of the authorities, and he was forced to leave Dámóc later in the 1920s or early '30s. During his exile, he married Serena Schoenberger and had three children. He and his family were deported from Nyíregyháza to Auschwitz, with the exception of his son Mordkha, who was visiting Dámóc at the time of his deportation. Separated from his wife and children, Dezso was soon sent to Buchenwald. He and his entire family were lost in the Shoah.

Szeren and Etel Perlstein were matched through arranged marriages in the 1930s with widowers, who were responsible for children in their care. Hearing about their arranged marriages from my mother, I wondered whether most of the marriages in my mother's ancestry had been similarly arranged or whether love matches were possible in their remote, rural part of the country, where available Jewish spouses may have been less numerous. The two moved to live with their spouses and stepchildren, Szeren to Kisvarda and Etel to Sátoraljaújhely, but Szeren left her husband and returned home to her family in Dámóc a few years later, placing her in the town at the time of her deportation.

Laura and Sidonia, Simon's youngest children, remained unmarried and continued to live and work in Dámóc. They were deported to Auschwitz in 1944, along with every other member of their extended family.

I would be remiss if I did not mention the Klein side of my mother's ancestral family. My grandmother Hani's family came from the wine-growing town of Karolyfalva, also in the northeastern sector of Hungary, not too far from Dámóc, located in one of the most arable regions of the country. The few distant cousins I had growing up and whom I still very much cherish emanated from this lineage.

The Kleins were steeped in viniculture as far back as they could remember. They lived and breathed the planting, cultivation, and harvesting of grapes that produced some of the finest white wines in the world. As my mother told the story, German aristocrats originally owned the vineyards. However, after members of the Klein family had devotedly operated the vineyards for years, they were apparently allowed to own their own piece of the land, and proudly tended it for the next several generations.

The documented Klein dynasty appeared to have begun with my great-great-grandfather David Klein and his wife Julia (sometimes referred to as Leni) Rubin. They had at least six children, Vincze (often referred to by his Hebrew name, Pinkasz),

Herman, Isaac, Bernat, Mihaly (sometimes listed as Karoly), and Eszter. In the 1869 census, the matriarch, Julia, born in 1818, appeared to be a widow and was living in the same household as my great-grandfather Vincze, born in 1847, and his wife Fani Guttman, along with Vincze's siblings Bernat, Eszter, and Karoly (probably Mihaly).

The only ancestral photograph. The author's great-granduncle Bernat's widow, Mari Lichtman Klein, surrounded by some of her family, 1922. The photo includes Eleanor before she immigrated to America, standing second from the left.

Later, one of Vincze's brothers, Isaac, moved to California before the turn of the twentieth century and became wealthy and prominent in the fur business, creating considerable gossip for the rest of his Hungarian Klein relatives in his home country. When my mother first arrived in America, she searched for and contacted Isaac's descendants in Beverly Hills. For their own reasons, they declined to help her. Fortunately, Sidonia found the descendants of another of Vincze's brothers, her granduncle Bernat, in New York. Although they were not nearly as wealthy, they provided her with the familial nurturing she so desperately needed.

As a child, I never knew how these cousins were related to my mother, but I remember our visits to the Bronx as some of the happiest moments of my childhood. How I loved the animated Hungarian exchanges between my mother and these cousins, whose matriarchs were Eleanor and Regina, Hani's first cousins. They were fortunate to have immigrated to America earlier in the twentieth century, unwittingly leaving behind the rest of their family to meet their ultimate doom.

Vincze and Fani bore at least eight children, but sadly, they also appeared to have lost four of them either in their infancy or prior to the age of two. Their surviving children into adulthood, my grandmother Hani, who may have been the oldest, Zali, Regina, and Marcusz, appeared to have remained in Karolyfalva at least until their marriages. All of them had spouses and multiple children. My few contemporary Klein relatives, my second and third cousins, all descended from David and Julia, either through one of Vincze's siblings or his offspring,

Hani was diagnosed with breast cancer in the mid-1930s. After a mastectomy and recuperation in a convalescent home in Debrecen, she did not live very much longer, passing away in 1936. She and my mother's sister Margit were the only members of their nuclear family buried in the tiny Jewish cemetery in Dámóc, which we saw during our visit. The rest of Hani's siblings and large extended family were all deported and, except for a handful of those in my mother's generation, perished in the Holocaust. Hani was spared the experience of losing her husband and all of her descendants, with the lone exception of Sidonia.

Although it would be impossible to know with any certainty the number of all those who perished during the Shoah in the extended Perlstein and Klein families, given their numerous progeny, it must have been exceedingly high.

Klein cousins, Melanie Hall and Chana Cromer, at the author's wedding, December 1969

I gained considerable solace from remembering my lost relatives and tracing their journeys through the Hungarian countryside. Despite the inevitable conflicting data I sometimes confronted on the genealogical websites regarding the spelling and variations of names, dates of birth and death, and missing threads of time, I found enough to understand the path of my maternal lineage. Combined with my mother's stories of her Hungarian life, I learned enough to know this: the Perlsteins and Kleins would have been proud to know that my mother inherited the entrepreneurial, managerial, industrial, creative, and interactive skills of her ancestors. Like them, she forged a different path than those around her, yet she also knew how to capitalize on her talents and assets to make her mark on the world.

As Henry's wife, Sidonia was popular among the Jewish women of Springfield and Longmeadow. They admired her keen intellect, creativity, and kindness and wanted her participation in their organizations. She loved joining in on planning of special community events to mark Jewish holidays, like the Jewish New Year, Passover, Purim, and Shevuot, the holiday commemorating the giving of the Torah.

Although she and Henry were not religiously active in their orthodox synagogue, they could always be counted on to provide donations to special causes or to lead committees formed to raise funds for the State of Israel, children and families in need, or to promote social justice efforts. Their store, Sid's Place, had provided for an excellent living and they wished to share their wealth with those less advantaged. They were sought-after guests at dinners, parties, charity events, and game nights.

Tutored by Sidonia, Henry joined her in becoming an expert domino player, picking up variations to the game and amusing his fellow players with his proficiency. She had played dominoes, a favorite family game in Hungary, since she was a young child. Moreover, she had observed German officers playing it in the castle she helped to maintain as a slave laborer at the Dachau concentration camp. She always marveled at how universal the game of dominoes could be, played during war and also in peace. The rules and strategies of the game had never left her. She was happy that Henry was equally as interested in playing since they made a formidable couple when they participated as a pair in dominoes games or tournaments. They were almost impossible to beat.

Sidonia had decided soon after coming to America that she never wanted to return to her home village or country. If the country could deport almost all of its Jewish citizens, despite their loyalty over hundreds of years and even serving as soldiers during World War I, in which her brother had been an infantryman, she had no compulsion to return to it. She could not stop remembering her loved ones or the setting of her upbringing, but her family was gone and she did not feel a need to see any of her neighbors who remained. Henry understood and commiserated with her feelings.

In America, Sidonia seemed skilled at everything she attempted, not only designing and creating beautiful clothing, but also serving up delicious cooked delicacies. The couple would often entertain at their home for a weekend lunch or dinner, when Sidonia would serve dishes such as authentic Hungarian goulash or the dumpling concoction called szilvas gomboc. *Since few Americans had ever tasted this Hungarian plum recipe, it was an instant hit with everyone who attended their mealtime feasts.*

Sidonia's life with Henry was as full, joyous, and active as she had hoped it would be after her arrival in America.

CHAPTER 23

Tension of Thread

> Tension of thread is regulated for needle-thread by tension dial, for bobbin thread by screw on bobbin case. Today's fabrics call for rather loose thread loops. Too tight tension causes puckered seams. —"Machine-stitching," page 116

Starting from when the children were four and ten years old, my family took a summer vacation each year, usually to Newport, Rhode Island and later to Cape Cod, where we stayed for one or two weeks. It seemed natural to take my mother with us. She did not have any other family or many friends, certainly none who would have invited her to vacation with them. I just assumed it was my role to always have her join our family. No matter how cumbersome it would become, I had no second thoughts. This was a mistake.

As the children grew older and more active, my mother had a hard time adjusting to the level of chaos that sometimes occurred on vacation. She could count on a lot of road travel, loud voices in the back of the car, unpacking at a hotel or resort, repacking, swimming in the pool or ocean, walking on the beach, going out to eat, and a host of other activities. She mumbled and grumbled under her breath for most of it.

> "Hani, vhere did Stevie go? *Gott my* [my God], I don't see him now," she asked with an anguished face when my son was three or four years old, desperately looking around her.

"Ma, he's behind you. He is trying to climb up the lifeguard's chair. I'll go after him."

"Oy, dis is such a problem mit dese kits! I can't keep track of dem," she shouted in an exasperated tone.

"I know, Ma. It's not easy, but we have to stay as calm as possible."

"Oy, Stevie, Stevie, vait dere till mommy can get you. Hani, he is really a *rossz kutya*!"

"Don't worry, Ma. I'll get him down," I said, trying to soothe her nerves.

Sidonia and her grandson in Newport soon after the lifeguard chair incident

I remembered that Hungarian phrase she used when I was a child and sometimes behaved badly. She called me a *rossz kutya*, which I was sure meant "wicked devil," or perhaps "evil satan." I never asked her what it actually meant, but when I heard this phrase again, I looked it up in my Hungarian dictionary. It meant "naughty dog." Not as bad as I thought.

Staying calm when surrounded by chaos or a flurry of people and activity was not something my mother was able to handle by the time she had grandchildren. She could manage me, most of the time, when I was the only child in her family. Once I was married and had young children of my own, the environment proved overwhelming for her.

I realize now that the memory of losing her entire family must have been a constant internal source of tension. Her loved ones were gone in what seemed like an instant and it was an occurrence beyond her control. The lines, the crowds, the selections, the dogs, the gas chambers, the disease, the starvation, the hard labor, the fear, the death, and the sudden loneliness when it was over: how could that ever have left her mind? When she was confronted with even a little confusion and innocent bedlam, those memories could not help but erupt and come to the surface. She could stand just so much of it.

That, among other things, must have been why she kept to herself for as long as I knew her, with the exception of interacting with her fellow factory workers earlier in her American life, her dressmaking customers, an occasional friend, and her family.

Taking annual vacations with my active children was too much for my mother. Including her on shorter and infrequent family trips would have been a much better choice for both her and my family.

CHAPTER 24

Buttons

> Buttons, with their companion buttonholes, generally serve as fastenings. They are also, with or without buttonholes, used as decoration ... Buttons may be made of almost any material—wood, metal, mother of pearl ... and in many shapes. They may be plain or fancy, worth a fortune ... or sold at a quarter a dozen.
> —"Buttons," page 42

She had taken to calling me "doll," a word she had adopted from one of her loyal dressmaking customers. I never complained but it seemed disingenuous for a woman who rarely used American slang or overly endearing words to refer to me as "doll." I realized that her customers, whose number continued to grow in the 1970s and '80s, began to play an even greater role in her life.

Since I had not lived at home with her for more than a decade, we saw each other mostly on weekends, when she drove her car, by then her second one, an olive green and cream-colored Oldsmobile Cutlass, to my home in Connecticut for the day.

These women had taken my place, at least in terms of offering my mother company, during what must have been an intensely lonely time. Their design and alteration requests kept her curious and challenged, a perfect antidote for loneliness. I recalled that it was this group of customers that arranged a wedding shower for me prior to my marriage. Although the shower was cancelled at the last minute due to inclement weather, I used the cutlery set for twelve that the group had purchased for me for many years thereafter.

The main characters in her life at this time were those who shared their desires, life experiences, body insecurities, and personal stories in the form of their clothing needs and wishes. She was proud of her role in their lives, whether it was altering a clothing item for better fit or creating a bold new design that they would never have found in stores. Of course, the garments would fit them perfectly. Sometimes it was the first time a customer owned a garment that really suited her due to her shape or size.

Havoc in Sidonia's busy sewing room

Like other personal services, dressmaking is an intimate occupation, putting the dressmaker in close proximity to the assets and deficits not only of each customer's body but often also those of her personal life. My mother acquired a good ear for listening to her patrons' personal stories, like the woman who needed specialized clothing for her disabled daughter, the one who needed an elegant dress for her anniversary, or the plus-size woman who struggled to find the right wardrobe. Once, she added sleeves and a bow to a neighbor's wedding dress for free, making it the ideal gown that the young woman could never afford. Sidonia found solutions for them all.

If she ever had what could be termed a friend, it would have been among this varied group of devoted customers, many of whom were blessed with affluence, but some who were more economically challenged and just in need of clothes that fit. Occasionally, Sidonia was invited to a wedding or Bar Mitzvah or other special occasion. At other times, a customer might have asked her to have lunch at a restaurant, something she had never done before, except with me.

I could see that she felt more comfortable with this set of women than she had ever been with any other group in America, even *di grine*, the immigrant group that formed our initial community after our arrival. Her customers would often share with me that my mother was very caring and empathetic to their needs and how much they enjoyed spending time with her. They confided that she talked about me incessantly. I wondered whether she, in turn, had shared her inner thoughts with any of them. Most likely, her pleasant conversation, although genuine, was, like her talent, also an exquisite cover for her painful secrets. Yet it showed that she possessed a social side to her personality that otherwise had rarely been on display.

"Hi doll," she responded, when I called her on the phone during my lunch hour. "It's nice to talk to you, but I very busy right now. Mrs. Frome, you know, she own da art gallery downtown. She is my favorite customer, Hani. She is taking me to lunch. Call me later. Bye." I sensed just a slight hint of exuberance in her voice.

"Oh, all right, Ma. Have a good time," I said, as I hung up, a bit off guard and wondering if this person on the phone was really my mother.

When I called her later in the evening, she told me about her lunch, but then added, "Hani, I so busy. I have so many deadlines today. I promised I vould have dem ready by da end of da veek. So I can't talk too long. But, let me ask you, how da kits?" She could not allow a conversation to end without asking about her grandchildren.

"I'm glad you had a good lunch, Ma. I know all about deadlines and they can be nerve-racking, but I'm sure you'll meet them. The kids are fine. I'll talk to you tomorrow." Later, I thought to myself that my mother sounded just like any other American businessperson whose world included customers and deadlines! I feared that she was experiencing too much stress but I also knew she thrived on the challenge.

Sidonia's sons, David and Martin, were devoted to their parents. Yet, their personal lives began to diverge from one another starting with high school. Less than a decade after Yale ended its Jewish quotas for admission, the college accepted David, the valedictorian of his class, as a pre-medicine student, where he continued to excel in his studies. He was later accepted to the Yale School of Medicine and then became an intern and resident at the Yale New Haven Hospital, specializing in pediatrics. By 1980, he had married a fellow doctor, Sarah, who gave birth to their first child, a son named Vincent. After a few years, he partnered with a fellow Yale Medical School graduate in opening a new pediatric practice in Springfield, which quickly gained prominence in the field of childhood cancer.

David's brother, Martin, did not fare nearly as well. Although his dyslexia was diagnosed in high school, he continued to have difficulty keeping up with his class in most subjects. All the years that his learning disability had gone undiagnosed had taken their toll on his academic success. His teachers felt that he could not succeed in college and recommended that he attend a vocational school or seek employment. Sidonia and Henry's sweet, loving, once-congenial son seemed to have few options when he graduated from high school. They found a job for him as a dishwasher in a local restaurant until he could devise a better plan for his future.

Martin began to drink heavily and could not seem to find his place in society. He left the dishwashing position and took on a series of odd jobs, always feeling that he did not fit in anywhere. Along the way, he added heroin to his daily habit. He often drifted from town to town, occasionally finding himself in a relationship with a woman he met on the road, but never finding happiness with any of them.

Sidonia and Henry were heartbroken about Martin's dismal life circumstances. They tried to remain in touch with him as much as possible, but his transiency made their efforts nearly impossible. When he would come back to his parents' home, Martin was usually jobless and would often ask his parents for money. They always complied, trying to remain a safe zone for their son.

As Martin neared forty and continued his life of addiction and instability, Sidonia and Henry decided to confront him with an intervention. They asked his brother and sister-in-law and a few friends who had kept in touch with him since high school to come to their home and meet with Martin about his addiction and erratic living conditions. After a period of planning, they were ready to honestly talk to Martin about how his addiction had affected their lives and their relationships with him. As she had never been part of any such confrontation, Sidonia was racked with anxiety, but pressed forward in playing her part in the dramatic action necessary to point Martin in the right direction.

At the end of the calm but urgent pleas of his family and friends, Martin agreed to seek treatment. The intervention had been successful. Sidonia and Henry helped him sign into a residential rehabilitation program in Connecticut, both of them relieved that he had finally acceded to treatment. The first step in his recovery was set. Unfortunately, only three days after checking himself into the center, he was gone.

After a few days of searching for him with the police and calling all the hospitals in the area, Sidonia received the dreaded phone call that she hoped to never hear. The police had found Martin dead at a rooming house more than a hundred miles away. He had died of the overdose they had always feared.

CHAPTER 25

Check-List for Trouble Spots

> Common sewing machine failures usually have a simple explanation. Check the following in the cases indicated: **Thread breakage**—Improper threading of either top or bobbin thread ... Started the machine with needle in incorrect position ... Tension too tight ... Rough spots on needle eye. **Irregular or skipped stitches**—Pressure too tight ... Pulling fabric. **Machine stuck**—Bits of thread stuck in bobbin case holder. **Needle breakage**—Wrong needle for machine ... wrong size needle for fabric ... Bobbin inserted incorrectly. —"Machine-Stitching," page 117

I have often thought about the comment my boss, Robert Weiss, the town manager of the Town of Manchester, made when I first began the job as human services director.

"You seem to lead a charmed life," he once said, after observing my family.

"Why do you say that?" I asked.

"Well, you have a good job, two beautiful children, a husband who works nearby, and a comfortable place to live. I'd say that's pretty charmed."

I did not want to dissuade him from his rosy opinion of my life so I just responded, "Oh, I see. I guess you could look at it that way."

In reality, my life was far from charmed. Although I was fortunate to have two great children and a place to live, my marriage continued to be on shaky ground during the '80s, as my career was shifting into high gear. My husband and I were just coasting during that decade, at a standstill about resolving our differences, and merely going through the motions of being a married couple. For a long time, neither of us wanted to take the initiative necessary to mend our relationship or to take any action that would decide the fate of our marriage.

Our children, Brenda and Stephen, were doing well at daycare and school. Brenda took ballet classes during that time, culminating in her appearance as one of the children in the opening act of The Nutcracker ballet. Her grades were good and her circle of friends was expansive. During most summers in the '80s, she had grown accustomed to spending days and overnights at Camp Shalom, a Jewish camp along Connecticut's Farmington River, eventually graduating from camper to counselor. She had become an insightful, sensitive child. Moreover, as opposed to my relationship with my own mother, which was marked by secrets, repression, and often miscommunication, Brenda and I had developed a close mother-daughter bond, in which each of us felt comfortable confiding in each other and sharing our thoughts, ideas, and life events.

Steve, six years younger, was developing into a digital master at a very young age. Before the age of ten, he had become interested in computer games and digital platforms. By the time he was twelve, in partnership with an equally precocious friend, he began to develop a digital bulletin board company, called Coral Reef, a forerunner of social media and information technology. I marveled at the entrepreneurial instincts of such a young person and his desire to stand out among his peers. I not only loved my son, but I genuinely admired his initiative. True to form, he preferred a computer camp to overnights at Camp Shalom.

During the '80s I focused on developing my career in the social work field. Manchester, a medium-income and diverse community, known as "the City of Village Charm," with a population nearing 60,000, was just the right place in which I could hone my skill at coordination and supervision. Teamwork, a concept that I had few opportunities to display until my Hartford job, became more important, not only in working with other department heads and community human services agencies, but also within my own department. I felt lucky that my coworkers were so collegial and willing to work together to promote the best services to the community—to recognize both our potential as a human service organization and the potential of the community we served, as well. It was a time when I felt the clearest about my profession, my problem-solving skills, my proficiency at working with others, and my ability to present and persuade. I had come into my own.

My confidence on the job helped to compensate for the troubles in my marriage. Like many working mothers, my job and homemaking responsibilities created moments of stress that, at times, seemed insurmountable. Devotion to my children's lives, schools, and activities in a climate of deep marital strife was a challenge that I navigated daily to the best of my ability. To this day, I am not certain how well I performed.

As the 1980s drew to a close, I realized that my inaction about my marriage stemmed from my desire to keep my family together no matter the cost. I had grown up in a fragmented family and did not wish to repeat that condition and pass it on to my own children. I did not want to be a single parent like my mother. As in all divorces, a separation would not only affect the spouses but the children and extended family. My husband's family had treated me as one of their own, and the thought of parting with them was difficult, as well. However, by the end of the decade, I knew that I would have to finally take some definitive action. The standoff could not continue. Although I wanted to keep my family intact and also assure my mother that I was in a stable family environment—something she wanted so much for me—I could no longer maintain the status quo.

To my surprise, my mother and my children already knew that I was in turmoil.

"Hani, I know den you are unhappy," my mother said to me one day.

"I'm sorry, Ma. I hoped that I could keep all my feelings inside and not alarm you or the kids."

"You know den you can't hide anyting fun me, just like I can't hide tings fun you. I can just look on your face and I know dat you are upset. I know dat tings mit your husband vasn't good for a long time."

Although I was sure that my mother and I had kept many things from each other my whole life, I overlooked her comment about not hiding things and responded, "Yes, one of us will have to do something about it soon. I'm just not sure what I am going to do."

Brenda and Stephen had also observed enough to understand that their parents had some problems that may have been irreparable. After a few futile sessions of marriage counseling, I asked for a divorce in 1990 and it was granted that August. I was officially a single parent with physical custodial rights to the children, but with co-parenting responsibilities.

As her father had trained my mother to be independent, so too did my mother train me. I had learned to handle my own finances during my marriage and had consistently held responsible occupations, placing me in a strong economic position to manage my family as a single mother. At the age of almost forty-three, with a great deal of my life still ahead, I said to myself, *So much for my charmed life. Now what?*

After my divorce, the 1990s brought the most stunning garments my mother had ever produced. She made brilliant ensembles for my work, including a white waffle-weave cotton embroidered jacket with blue flowers and matching white skirt, a three-piece floral-patterned skirt and top with solid lavender jacket, a magenta glen plaid wool collarless jacket with black wool

The author wearing the windowpane check suit meeting Eddie Fisher, 1995

lightweight paisley jacket and skirt, and a warm red cotton jacket and skirt. Then, there was that light brown windowpane check collarless jacket with culottes that I wore to the fiftieth reunion of Holocaust survivors at Miami's Fontainebleau Hotel, where I posed for pictures with the popular featured guest, Eddie Fisher, a television mainstay for survivors in the 1950s.

The author wearing the red cotton suit, with Beth Stafford, CEO of MACC Charities, Manchester, Conn., Flora Jimenez, director of Puerto De Fe (Port of Faith), Monica Pagan, and Kathryn Kirby, formerly of NBC CT 30

Leisure garments, some worn at work and some worn for outside activities, dotted my wardrobe and Brenda's, too, like matching vests and skirts in cotton, wool, and velvet. Occasionally, my mother included a hand-made matching fabric belt with a vest ensemble. Of course, all her designs included lace seam binding at the hem edge of every skirt or pants to add extra beauty even on the inside of the garment. It was as though she had to find and create beauty to cover up the ugliness she had endured in her past. Her intimate work with textiles of all kinds gave her an understanding that most of us could never possess—one described by writer Virginia Postrel as recognizing the important part textile played in the development of "the phenomenon we call civilization."

*Brenda's interchangeable blue suit, the jacket and skirt.
Also includes a vest and pants not shown.*

In 1993, Sidonia created inspired suits and dresses for Steve's Bar Mitzvah, both for the morning service and evening reception, which caused a sensation among invited guests and others who heard about the designs. For daytime, she created similar cream-colored day dress suits for both Brenda and me with different lace trims and fasteners. For evening, she fabricated black evening dresses, mine of a faux silk polyester with chiffon sleeves combined with a gold lame shawl, and Brenda's with polyester and lace sleeves.

The author and Brenda wearing their cream-colored suits trimmed with lace

Brenda's black Bar Mitzvah dress with lace sleeves

It was hard to fathom that my mother, during her period of highest design couture, was in her late seventies and eighties.

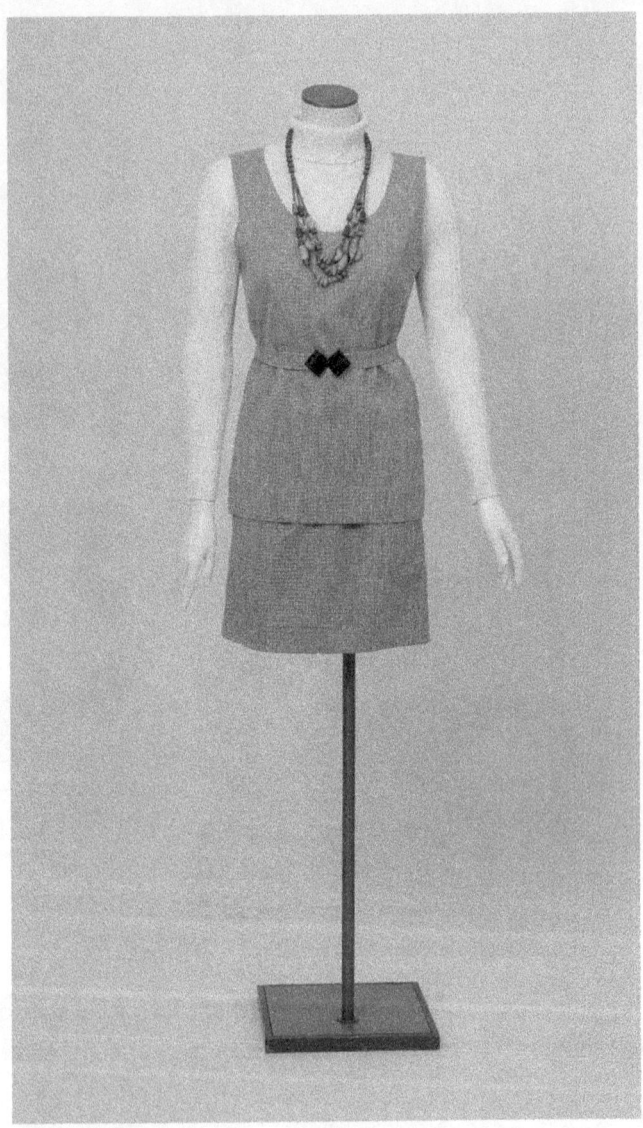

Brenda's houndstooth vest and skirt

CHAPTER 26

Zippers

> Zippers are another of those things that scare a home sewer. Yet inserting a zipper takes no particular skill or practice. There's a trick to it, of course, but it is by no means a difficult trick once you know what the motions are (i.e., once you have followed through on them) ... The motions are simple—if the instructions are lengthy, it is because we do not want to leave you with questions in your mind. — "Zippers," page 172

June 1993. It was 11:30 a.m., or 6:30 p.m. Israeli time. We had to leave soon for a long car ride and ferry to a town in New York to attend a Bar Mitzvah. Yet, I was adamant that I wanted to make this phone call before I left. I was not sure why I chose that day, but once I was intent on making it, I could not turn back.

"Brenda, I think I need a witness for this call," I said to my daughter. "Could you pick up the extension and listen? Please don't say a word, though," I warned, as she tacitly nodded her head, already knowing what I was about to do. Then, I dialed the number I had researched. After the woman who answered told him he had a caller, my father eventually came to the phone and we had a momentous but discouraging conversation, which I have recounted at greater length in a previous volume. This conversation, along with my Hungarian trip a decade earlier, profoundly changed my relationship with my mother.

My father seemed cordial during the conversation, asking how my mother was and vocalizing his strong attachment to Israel, despite having lived in New York City for a number of years after his immigration from Germany. He had married a Czech woman, had another daughter, and moved to Israel in the 1970s. He had not told a soul about my existence. Sure, he would like to have my address, he said, and maybe we could correspond, although I could tell he had no intention of doing so.

It was all very civil, yet guarded. He did not dispute in any way the fact that he was my father nor did he question why I was calling. Perhaps he had been expecting me to contact him at any time in the previous forty years and this was the awaited call. He did not know how my life had evolved up to that point, whether I had fared well in life or had suffered emotionally or physically during his long absence. Judging by his muffled, hushed tone, he was obviously hoping no one nearby could hear him. I could tell he was nervous.

As a child, I may have briefly imagined that my father was a kind man who sincerely wanted to remain in my life but was thwarted by my mother. However, as an adult, I could invent no alternative reality for him. I had gleaned from pieces of correspondence I had uncovered that he wanted to put the liaison and child firmly in his past. As one of his relatives wrote to my mother in my infancy, *"even though he has made a mistake too ... you cannot expect him to be unfortunate his whole life ... why did you not get an abortion in time?"* I had to assume that my father felt that way, too.

After the phone discussion, I realized that my father still did not want me in his life. He had not changed his view since the time of my birth. That was his reality: he had made a mistake as a teenager and he did not want to pay for it forever. Still, I had the distinct feeling that he had paid for it mentally for the rest of his life. He had not forgotten about his first child. The two-minute conversation monopolized my thoughts during the ferry ride to New York and for many years thereafter.

I wrestled with telling my mother that I had talked with my father. I wondered if, at long last, it was time to bring matters of my conception into open discussion. Ultimately, I decided against it. She had tried so hard to keep it from me for the previous forty-five years. She must have had her reasons, some having to do with shame and resentment, but by that time, I realized it was more for protective reasons. She loved me so much that she did not want anything to prevent me from possessing the positive self-image she desired for me.

After my phone conversation with my father, I began to tell my mother that I loved her unconditionally.

> "You know, Ma. There is nothing you can say or do that would ever stop me from loving you," I told her many times in the following years.
> "Yeh, Hani. I love you, too."

Earlier in my life she did not often tell me that she loved me. Her actions articulated her loving feelings more than her words. It was in the last dozen years of her life that she vocalized the sentiment more than ever, almost as though she had an instinct that I had discovered something about her and my father, and was relieved that I still loved her.

CHAPTER 27

One-Way Design

> Your pattern envelope will tell you what **type of fabric** is suitable and what **amount** you will need. You will note that yardages indicated are always specified "without nap" or "with nap." "With nap" takes a little more fabric because, nap running in one lengthwise direction, the pattern pieces will all have to be laid out with their top edges facing the same way. "Nap" however, does not cover the situation. Any fabric that looks different when held up or down has the same requirement. This means that the *design* ... may go in one direction, or the *weave* ... reflects light differently ... or the *texture* ... looks different. —"Fabrics," page 70

In many ways, I favor the loner lifestyle. I do not have to share or compromise very much. I choose when and where I want to go, what to purchase, my food, my commitments, and my secrets. Even though I lived with my mother for my first twenty or so years and loved her in my own way, we also lived separate lives, particularly after my college years. In addition, my failed marriage meant that I was often alone, although I had my children at home to love and adore until they were adults. With the divorce, I became the only adult in our household. When the children went off to college, married, and moved to other locations, I became even more alone, but by that point, it was my preferred mode of living.

However, the human species was not meant to live totally alone, and I have always sought someone to keep me company, love me, and offer solace, validation, and most importantly, humor.

In opposition to my childhood experience, I seek moments of laughter. As much as I desired isolation, I also have relished romance and interaction with someone else, albeit with a modicum of alone time.

As a woman of secrets, although not thoroughly hidden from those closest to me, I would never recount the details of romantic relationships I have had in the thirty years since my divorce. Although never a serial dater, I have had a few male connections over the years, usually long-term. These relationships have met my need for companionship and affection and I have given warmth and affection in return.

After my divorce, however, I was no longer interested in the concepts of compromise or outright deference of one person to the other. Acquiescence to the wishes of my mother had been a way of life for me, but I could no longer do the same for a man. Starting in my middle age, I seemed to prefer being independent. The two constant exceptions to my solitary existence have been the true friendships I have developed and the small family I created.

My mother lived most of her American life without the closeness of friendship. She had difficulty learning how to be a friend, which required some effort and commitment on her part. She preferred going in her own direction by herself. Maybe her reticence and shame about her past combined with her reclusive living circumstances kept her from fully dedicating herself to friendship. Whenever I think of my mother, I always visualize her standing alone, the most solitary being I have ever known.

In contrast, although my loner instincts have probably kept me from making some friends, I realized as a child that great friendships would act as my extended family, taking the place of the one that had been brutally taken from me. I also knew that if I were to have great friendships, I would have to be a great friend, to both men and women. That was what I strived to be all these years to my peers among *di grine*, my work colleagues, and synagogue pals.

Young adult and teen Brenda and Stephen with their grandmother

My early childhood friends among my *grine* community, whom I met when I was five years of age, have always meant a great deal to me. Our shared upbringing, our common backgrounds, and the distinct sense of our parents' suffering have bound us together for life. Long-term friendships that developed during my work in Hartford and Manchester have also sustained me and provided a social outlet of like-minded health and human services devotees, steeped in public service. Their insight, creativity, and humor have been indispensable. My synagogue friends, with whom I share faith and mutual respect, have always been comforting and supportive. They all have comprised my extended family.

As for my own family, looking back, I do not know why I ever hesitated to have children. Without them and their spouses and offspring, I would have been bereft of any close family. They have continued to offer me their love and understanding before and ever since the day of my divorce. I have needed them to check on my physical and mental soundness; to share my mostly mundane daily events and to hear about theirs; to keep me abreast of and include me in their own family happenings; and to understand and appreciate the history of our mutual lost ancestors.

Life without Brenda, Stephen, and their families would have been unbearable.

CHAPTER 28

Gussets

> A gusset is a small three- or four-cornered piece of fabric inserted into a slash to provide ease ... The point of an underarm slash is subjected to considerable strain, and since there is no seam allowance there, the gusset is liable to pull out. It is extremely important, therefore, to reinforce point of slash before inserting gusset. —"Gussets," pages 93–94

I had not seen Rabbi David Edelman, my childhood rabbi, in more than twenty-five years when we met again in the mid-1990s. My life had taken me in a direction that veered from the strict orthodoxy of my early childhood, when I was a student at the Lubavitcher Yeshiva School, where he was the principal. I idolized him then. His abundant beard, slim figure, wide smile, dark fedora hat, and long coat fascinated me. He was the perfect unattainable father figure with a wife and a multitude of children.

We met on a cloudy June morning in 1996 at a graveside funeral service in Connecticut. Coincidentally, the deceased had been a mutual friend, someone who had been on the governing body of the Connecticut town in which I worked, and also a member of a rural synagogue not far from Springfield in which Rabbi Edelman had taken special interest. By all accounts, it was an odd place to meet.

I saw him from afar, looking astonishingly the same as I remembered from my youth, with the exception of some gray strands sprinkled throughout his dark hair and bountiful beard. I wondered whether I should approach him to say hello. Even though so many years had elapsed since I had last seen him, I retained a sense of awe about him and I was not sure he would remember me, a student from so long ago, now standing before him in my crisp homemade double-breasted black polished cotton suit. Yet, already knowing my answer, I walked toward him after the funeral service ended. Drawing closer to him, I instinctively stretched out my right arm, with the intent of introducing myself and firmly shaking his hand, as I normally would with a work colleague.

As I got closer, I saw him stare intently at my outstretched arm. With his arms behind his back, he said, "Chana (the version of my name beginning with the guttural sound), it's so nice to see you. How are you doing?"

I looked up at his face and immediately pulled my arm down to my side. *What was I doing? Didn't I remember that he would never have shaken my hand or even touched it? A strictly orthodox Jew would never touch a woman other than his own wife. What was wrong with me?*

"I'm doing fine, Rabbi," I responded quickly. "I'm so sorry we had to meet on this very sad occasion. I wasn't sure if you would recognize me."

"Of course I would remember one of my best students." Having heard that I had married and borne children, he asked, "How are your husband and your children? I hope you are raising them in a Jewish way, with *Yiddishkeit*."

"My children are doing fine. I have a son and daughter who are growing really fast. My son just recently had his Bar Mitzvah. I have some bad news about my husband, though. We were divorced a few years ago."

He took a long step backwards as though he had been powerfully struck in the *kishkes* [guts] and had lost his footing. "You mean you are now alone?" he asked, almost reeling.

"Yes, I am," I responded, feeling a bit cornered by his unexpected and visible disappointment with me.

He lowered his voice just a little, while coming closer, and said, "You must remarry as soon as possible. A Jewish woman shouldn't be without a husband. It isn't right."

I wondered whether he remembered that my mother had been just that, a Jewish woman with a child and with no husband. Maybe he had given her the same cautionary advice at some point earlier in her life and was dismayed to see me following in her footsteps.

Not really sure what to say in response, I began to open my mouth to speak anyway. At that moment, a co-worker, sensing my distress, clasped my arm and pulled me away. "There's someone who wants to see you right now," she said. I muttered a quick goodbye and walked away, not even looking back at him. I sensed that the Rabbi was still in the same spot watching me, probably wondering how I could have gone so astray.

I only saw him for a couple of fleeting moments after that, at some event or other, notably at my mother's funeral in Springfield about a decade later. Ironically, we were at a cemetery again when he approached me as I was walking to my car after the service. He brought up his remembrances of my tendency to doodle at my desk when I was a student at his school. "Do you remember? I bought you special crayons and paper because I wanted to encourage your artistic talent," he said. Remarkably, he had recalled the nervous habit of drawing flowers and trees that I exhibited at six and seven years old. The subject of my marital status never came up.

Nevertheless, I dwelled upon our previous discussion. How could I not, when a man of such high esteem, who commanded my utmost admiration and respect, offered cautionary counsel about my marital condition? I did not forget his words, but neither did I follow them.

Sidonia and Henry mourned for their son, Martin, for the rest of their lives. They had given him as much love as any parents could provide for their child, but it was not enough. He had spiraled into an aimless life that was beyond their control to change. Although they had hoped their intervention would lead him to recovery, he was, unfortunately, not able to take advantage of their attempts at saving him.

In the 1990s, the couple sold Sid's Place to a family who promised to keep the name and continue to specialize in the leisurewear that Sidonia had promoted long before its eventual worldwide popularity. Customers continued to find their way to the store from miles around in order to purchase the informal women's clothing. Sidonia and Henry were confident that the store would continue to thrive under new ownership.

In their new free time, Sidonia and Henry traveled to Israel, Italy, England, and Canada to experience the sights and cultures of other lands. When they were home, they spent time with their son, David, who had become a prominent specialist in pediatric leukemia, and his wife, Sarah, and grandchildren, Vincent and Herman. As a family, they built a beach cottage on Cape Cod, where they all spent part of every summer, playing dominoes and solving puzzles, swimming in the sea or fishing in Cape Cod Bay. While the summers were hectic on the Cape, Sidonia was able to handle the bustling pace as long as she had Henry beside her. He was the steadying force who helped her retain her composure even when the noise, confusion, and innocent bedlam brought up reminders of her lost family at the moment of their annihilation.

They shared great pride in their son, David, who received numerous awards for his compassion and dedication to his patients and his service to children and families. He and Sarah, a fellow pediatrician, had a solid marriage and both had bustling practices. In addition, they followed the example of their parents by giving to various charitable causes in which they believed. For instance, David had seen the plight of many families faced with economic barriers to health care. After discussing his concerns with community members, he took the lead in creating a popular golf tournament to raise funds for patients unable to afford needed specialized care. Over many years of operating the tournament, he raised more dollars than he could have imagined. His parents had taught him well.

ALTHOUGH MY IMAGINARY fantasies about Sidonia's life included sadness in the form of losing one of her beloved sons, they also included a son who gave her reason for pride, satisfaction, and pleasure. It also allowed her to live a life with Henry of travel, recreation, romantic love, and personal fulfillment in a manner that eluded her in reality.

CHAPTER 29

Self-Fringe

> Self-fringe can be very chic, especially in woolens ... The fabric edge must be absolutely straight-grain. Draw out a thread along edge and trim edge evenly. Using a pin, draw out a thread at desired depth of fringe. Unless fabric is very firmly woven, make a line of machine-stitching, zigzag or straight, along that line. Beginning at stitched line, draw out threads (be sure to trim away first any selvage left in seams). — "Decoration," page 59

As we drove onto the campus of Eastern Connecticut State University, my family was excited about the ceremony in honor of my award as Humanitarian of the Year, 2000. My mother was grinning from ear to ear in the back seat of the car. She had told everyone she knew in Springfield that her daughter was earning her doctorate and she was looking forward to seeing me receive my diploma. Telling her for what seemed like the hundredth time that I was not receiving my doctoral diploma but an award for my dedication and commitment to the field of substance abuse prevention, I could not change her thinking.

Noted as the first woman to attain the distinction by a well-known addiction service agency, I received considerable media attention and kudos from friends, family, and colleagues for the recognition. Yet, my mother's approval was the most important. No matter that she mistook my award for something else. She was happy and that was enough.

"Hani, in vhat subject are you getting your doctor degree?" she asked before we arrived. "I forgot."

"Ma, I would like to have a doctorate but this is an event to honor me for my work. The ceremony will be at a college, but I'm not a student there. They're recognizing me for all my work through my job in the community."

"Okay, Hani. I got it. But all dis time, I tink you vorking on your doctor degree."

"I know, Ma, but believe me, this award is a big deal."

"I alvays proud of you, Hani."

I knew that was the truth.

My mother was then eighty-seven years old, and although she had not by a long shot ceased to create and sew, she had slowed down a bit. Sometimes she allowed me to wear attire that I had purchased in an actual store rather than one of her homemade designs. In 2000, she allowed it twice. At the award ceremony, I wore a two-tone polyester dress, featuring a deep red bodice, separated from the solid black straight skirt by an embedded print belt, accompanied by a short red bolero jacket with black single lapel. It felt strange wearing clothing that my mother had not made for me, but at the same time, slightly liberating. Still, it was not lost on me that the ensemble also had no lining or pockets, missing some of the hallmarks of my mother's fashions.

In August that year, my daughter, Brenda, turned twenty-six and married her husband, Michael, in a large wedding ceremony and reception. My mother not only encouraged me to wear a store-bought gown, but she was amenable to having me pick out a dress for her, as well.

Her flow of steady design output had diminished since she had moved to an elderly housing development two years earlier. She no longer had a dedicated sewing room where she kept all

Receiving the Humanitarian of the Year Award from Leanne Dillian, Executive Director, Community Prevention and Addiction Services

her equipment, including her machine, iron and ironing board, garment rack, cutting table, and fabric storage area. Her sewing machine, still the Pfaff, was set in front of a wall in her small living room, while other supplies were relegated to different locations in her apartment. Moreover, it was uncomfortable for customers to come to an elderly housing development instead of a private residence, which reduced the number of garments she created and altered.

Moving to a new home was a difficult adjustment that was offset by Sidonia's contentment at saving rental costs in subsidized housing, but her tendency toward self-seclusion seemed to increase with fewer customers and smaller living quarters. Luckily, she still had ideas about sewing projects and continued to make special garments for my work and leisure as well as outfits for Brenda.

A fringe benefit of not having as many traditional customers was free time to focus on her new project: cloth "baggies." In order to keep herself busy at all times, she turned to creating handmade flowered and solid-colored bags in all sizes, fabrics, and shapes.

> "Hani, dese little bags are such a good idea. Dey so easy to make and people really love dem. I give dem avay to ladies I like and who are so nice to me."
>
> "I know you're fussy about who receives one of your bags, though, Ma."
>
> "Maybe, Han, but I vant to show dem I preciate how dey helped me," she replied, leaving off the "a" in "appreciate," as usual. "I tink I made more den von hundert already."
>
> "Yeah, Ma. I have quite a few of your bags, too, and I love them. I keep my makeup, jewelry, change, and even some wallet photos in them. I don't know what I'd do without them now."
>
> "I gonna make dem as long as I can do it," she said with sincerity.

Until her very old age, I noticed no difference in the quality of her work compared to her earlier years. Her passion for dressmaking and design had not waned. The sequence of creating a garment followed the same steps as always: imagining the full outfit in her mind; selecting a pattern; deciding what adjustments to the pattern were desired; determining what type of fabric was

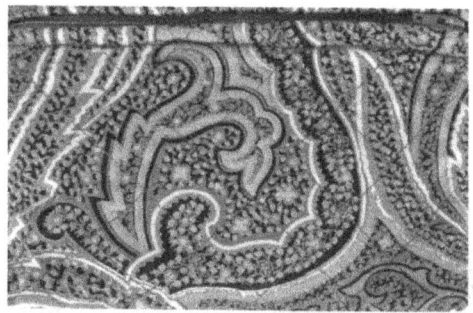

A brown print baggie

most suitable; cutting the pattern and fabric; basting, pinning, and sewing certain garment sections; doing fittings at several intervals; finishing final seams and edges; measuring and pinning the hemline; and sewing hems and finishing hem edges with seam binding. Finally, if the garment required it, an intensive hunt for just the right matching buttons ensued. To my amazement, the entire order of things, as though by rote, remained the same, but her sharp-edged mind began to dull.

At around the same time, the nearby Hatikvah [the Hebrew word for "hope"] Holocaust Education Center, then housed in an addition to the Springfield Jewish Community Center, asked her to share her Holocaust experiences with local students who visited the center. She had not shared any of her stories with anyone but me in the past, but realizing that she was in the twilight of her life, she responded in the affirmative. I believed that in her ninth decade, she knew that her experiences offered lessons to young people about the cruelty of oppression and the importance of acting as an upstander rather than a bystander when hate becomes pervasive. She wanted to tell them that she had a large family once and that they had actually lived and contributed to their community. Although nervous to do that which she had avoided for so long, she delivered quite a few lectures to not only students but to teachers, as well. I joined her a few times to boost her comfort level and to fill in events that she may have forgotten.

> "Yeh, I had a vonderful family mit tree sisters and a broder. I vill never forget dem. Dey vere all smarter den me," she said humbly to the students, evoking laughter to her self-deprecating humor. Her comment reminded me of the psychiatrist, author, and survivor Viktor Frankl's observation that those who survived may have used every means available in order to live. In his words, "the best of us did not return."
>
> "And all her sisters knew how to sew, too, just like her," I added. "We sometimes wonder what kind of beautiful garments they could have made if they had lived."

I could tell by the students' faces that they were struck by my mother's courage in conveying the details of her lost family. Her long-term memory was, indeed, intact. As she was not sure she could handle conveying the details of specific events in the concentration camps or the displaced persons camp, she wanted to talk more about her family and their contented life in Hungary before they were summarily extinguished from the face of the earth. She received the following letter, among others, from an appreciative coordinator of teacher training, who heard my mother speak in 1998:

> *Dear Mrs. Perlstein,*
> *Thank you so much for taking the time to speak to the teachers last week. I found the session extremely moving, and know that many of the participants felt the same way. I look forward to seeing you again and appreciate the help you gave us.*
> *Cheers,*
> *Jack, "Facing History and Ourselves"*

Sidonia in her late eighties

CHAPTER 30

Marking the Hemline

> The hemline is the line on which a hem is folded up (i.e., the finished edge of garment). It must be at the *right level*, and it must be *even*—that is, at the same distance from floor all around ... A **pattern** usually indicates depth of hem. If through measurement and past experience, or if you have altered the pattern to fit, you know you can use this hemline, proceed as for the **straight skirt**.
> —"Hems," page 99

My mother's behavior began to change somewhat in the mid-1990s, when she grew more anxious about minor things, even when the environment around her was calm. Sometimes she began to whine with frustration when things did not go her way, a phenomenon I had never observed in my youth. I made the mistake of not inviting her to Brenda's twenty-first birthday party because of her possible irritable behavior at night, a disrespectful decision which I still regret. She sensed my slight almost immediately and made sure that I was aware of her disapproval and hurt feelings. I had never done anything like that before and never did again.

In 2003, when my mother turned ninety and had completed her last full home-sewn suit, a spring flowered cotton print skirt and jacket, she changed all at once, as though someone had turned off a switch. In the previous year, she had lost her way driving to my house, a trip she had taken many times in the past, and then endured a serious accident with her car, the Buick Century, the last of her trio of automobiles during her forty years of driving. She veered a bit off to the side as she drove down a road not too far from her apartment and crashed into a parallel-parked vehicle. Not stopping to inform anyone in the house behind the parked car about the accident, she continued to drive until she returned home, where she called me in a panic.

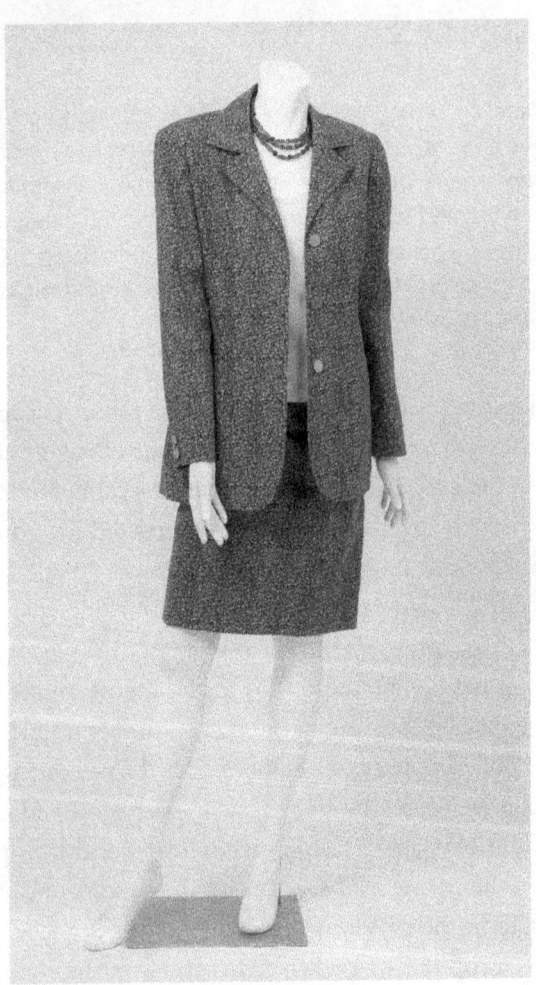

Sidonia's last spring cotton flowered suit

I quickly drove with her to the scene of the accident. After settling with the car's owners, I had her tested for her driving ability and regretfully concluded that she could no longer drive. Moreover, her car was too damaged to repair and I could not, in good conscience, allow her to replace it. The loss of her independence, represented in part by her vehicle, may have been the trigger for her subsequent steep mental and physical decline.

She began to walk in a twisted fashion, her right leg forming a half circle as it swung from back to front in her stride. She seemed even more reclusive and antisocial than ever. Relying on the senior bus to take her to a lunch site every day, she grew more and more impatient as she waited for the bus driver to pick her up and often walked in freezing temperatures and dense snow if the driver was just a few minutes late. She had earned just enough through her early factory work and her thirty-eight years of self-employment to afford all her needs without any help. She would have been willing to spend it all on a car that would have given her the independence she had grown to relish. But it was not to be.

I took her every weekend to do her grocery shopping, but she did not buy very much, mainly cottage cheese, jelly, and bread. My entreaties to her to come and live with me fell, as usual, on deaf ears. She felt most comfortable in the neighborhood and city in which she had spent most of her American life. She almost always remembered my name and that of other members of my family. However, a few months after her ninetieth birthday, after a short hospital stay and at her own request, she was admitted to the Jewish Nursing Home, no longer able to live on her own in her small apartment.

I have offered an account of my mother's three-year adventure in the nursing home previously when her basic obstinate, independent personality remained intact, but her cognitive powers became diminished. In essence, she reverted back to her Holocaust experiences when she viewed every piece of food as one to savor and retain in order to share or trade it with her bunkmates. In the concentration camps, it was a matter of survival. Sixty years later, as a nursing home resident, she remembered the instincts that had helped her live through the worst time of her life. With her appetite gone and her dentures too loose for her mouth, she saved as much as she could of her meals and accumulated them in used containers in her small dormitory-style refrigerator. Brenda or I made sure to remove them on our regular visits to the nursing home, pretending to take them home for our family's enjoyment.

The year, 2003, also marked the year that my mother's first great-granddaughter, Brenda's daughter, Lauren, was born. As a treat, I signed her out of the nursing home for a day to attend the baby's naming service at the synagogue and the reception that followed. The excitement of experiencing the extension of her family even further into the future was so visible that her face seemed transcendent in a constant smile, only to end upon her return to the nursing home.

An extreme example of my mother's need to save food items in her old age occurred when the Jewish Nursing Home invited families to join her and other residents for a communal Jewish New Year dinner. A large challah bread sat at the center of each table, but no one at ours ate the bread and it remained whole. When everyone else had left the table, my mother, who had been eyeing the bread throughout dinner, took the challah and wrapped it in a couple of napkins, preparing to take it back to her room.

> "Ma, why are you taking the challah? It's too much bread for just one person," I asked her, when I noticed the carefully wrapped loaf on her lap.
>
> "But maybe ve vant to eat it sometime," she brusquely stated.

Lauren's baby naming, 2003. Sidonia, Michael, Brenda, Steve, and the author, holding baby Lauren.

"No, Ma. We won't want to eat it. You should leave it on the table."

"Vell, Han. Dat is da difference betveen me an you. I know vhen ve should save food," she said, waving at me with her hand, as though to dismiss my objection.

I knew that I could not argue the issue with her. Her mind was made up. Before I left the nursing home, I helped her to tightly squeeze the large challah into her tiny refrigerator, only to remove it on my next visit.

In 2004, I took an early retirement from the Town of Manchester after twenty-four years. With mixed emotions, I left the job that had helped me fulfill the vision of my life's work; I was also leaving the friends that I had made along the way. I had earned my state licensure in clinical social work during my time there and hoped I could use it in the future to work in independent practice. Conveniently, the Town employed me on a part-time basis for another two years to help complete a capital project on which I had played a lead role.

My retirement meant I finally had the opportunity to spend more precious time with my mother. As she remained in the nursing home in Longmeadow, Massachusetts, with few visitors and a tendency to keep to herself, except for an occasional game of bingo, I vowed to see her as many days of the week as possible.

She had restless nights at the nursing home, constantly depriving her of much-needed sleep. Moreover, it seemed that the more medication she received for arthritic pain and sedation, the more her cognitive abilities decreased. At times, she slurred her words and begged for a wheelchair so that she would no longer require a walker, not realizing that once she made that transition, she would never walk again. We finally gave in to her pleas and allowed the nursing home staff to remove the walker and give her the desired wheelchair.

One time, but only one, she introduced me to someone as her cousin.

> "Dis is my cousin fun Hungary. She heard I vas here and came to visit me," she told an acquaintance in the nursing home's hallway.
>
> I sheepishly corrected her, "No, actually, I'm her daughter, Hanna, not her cousin. I grew up here in Springfield." Her introduction had caught me off guard since she had never confused my identity in the past.

The acquaintance just smiled and said nothing, observing the awkward moment. I should have just left it alone and not corrected her or drawn attention to her error. It was so hard to watch my strong, self-reliant mother sitting in a wheelchair, not knowing my name, and with no fabric or a needle and thread in her hands. To my relief, she never forgot who I was again.

Often when I visited, we would move to the home's activity room so we could be close to her Pfaff sewing machine, which had been moved there in case she wanted to use it. Even though her increasing dementia meant that she was no longer able to sew, she found solace when near her machine and sewing supplies. Since sewing was almost synonymous with breathing for her, each stitch synchronized with her heartbeat, I knew that she did not have much longer to live.

In the mid-1990s, when Henry was in his eighties, he began to exhibit the signs of dementia. Among other untypical behaviors, he began to show indications of some cognitive changes, like forgetting his medication for a heart arrhythmia, the names of his closest friends, basic microwave settings, and the directions to their favorite restaurant.

At first, these forgotten tasks were mild in nature. Sidonia watched over him closely now that they were retired and helped him to compose lists of names, directions, and daily tasks. During her life in America, she had become a voracious reader and student of the English language. She spoke with only a slightly noticeable accent and wrote using excellent spelling and sentence structure. Her writing skills came into play as she helped Henry compensate for his cognitive deficits.

They enjoyed eating out once or twice a week, attending functions in the Jewish community, and participating in David's charity golf tournaments. Henry could still play golf if someone else kept score, while Sidonia sold tickets to the events. She continued to cook her specialty meals while Henry washed the dishes. They were a team almost as much then as they had been earlier in their marriage.

A couple of years later, Sidonia detected that Henry's behavior was growing more erratic. He began to leave his car keys in the refrigerator, lost track of dates and time, and forgot the names of his children, often appearing anxious and disoriented. She was deeply concerned when Henry was diagnosed with Alzheimer's disease. As his ability to carry on his usual daily tasks diminished, Sidonia took on his responsibilities and monitored his progress.

One evening after dinner at home, Henry left the house while Sidonia was in the bathroom. Noticing his absence, Sidonia called his name inside and then outside of the house, but Henry did not reply. She knocked on her neighbors' doors looking for him, but no one had seen him. They sensed Sidonia's frazzled state and helped her to search for Henry. Soon, they found him, dressed in his pajamas. Sidonia's beloved Henry had died near a grove of trees close to his home.

Henry was so well known and respected in the community that many friends and neighbors reached out to console Sidonia. During the funeral service, attended by members of the community of all faiths, their son, David, spoke eloquently about his father's integrity and decency and the devotion he demonstrated to his mother. In a small section of his eulogy, he expressed his emotions in Yiddish.

After the funeral, Sidonia wondered how she would go on living without Henry. Although her own resilience and strength of character had helped her to continue life after the Holocaust, she had leaned on Henry for more than forty years to calm her and give her a feeling of safety. She had found her life's partner after she had lost everyone else she loved. Could she go on without him?

Sidonia sold their Longmeadow home after Henry's death and moved to a nearby condominium community. At age eighty-seven, she began to sew a little more often, finding herself instinctively *drawn to her sewing machine. Noticing images of flowered mini cloth bags in magazines, she created hundreds of colorful flowered bags of all sizes, fabrics, and shapes designed with various stitching. She delivered many of them to the local Jewish Family Services to distribute to clients in need at holiday time and often used them as special tokens of her appreciation for bank tellers, grocery clerks, lunch helpers, neighbors, and others who gave her a helping hand. After a while, many members of her community had a flowered bag handcrafted by Sidonia.*

Never one to speak aloud to anyone about her Holocaust experiences, she felt more open at that point in her life to talk to others, particularly students, about her life before and during that horrible period. The lessons of the Holocaust—the danger of hate, the power of human resilience, the importance of kindness, and the memories of those that were lost—were too important to keep to herself. She had a story that needed to be told. However, she still kept secret her ill-fated love affair during her stay at the displaced persons camp. She would never forget it, but it was a chapter of her life she could never reveal.

My imaginary mother, like her real-life counterpart, also embarked on a series of talks at Springfield's Hatikvah Holocaust Education Center, which invited local high school classes to come and hear survivors speak about their Holocaust story.

Sometimes David would join her, although he, himself, had not heard many of her tales due to her long-standing reluctance to speak of them to her family. As she grew more accustomed to public speaking, she became one of the most popular speakers at the center, interacting with hundreds of students, who hung on to her every word. Sidonia had found meaning in her life after Henry.

AS THE IMAGINARY version of Sidonia continued to age along with the real Sidonia, they shared similar experiences. They were magnetically drawn to the sewing machine, made small items like baggies, and were compelled to tell a little more of their past history to those who wanted to learn from their experiences. Indeed, the imaginary Sidonia and my real mother were the same woman, separated only by a single turn of events that changed the trajectory of their lives.

CHAPTER 31

Fabric Finishes

> All commercial fabrics ... are processed with a finish when they come from the loom. These finishes in the course of application frequently pull the crosswise threads out of line ... the only ones of importance to us are the permanent finishes ... these finishes have a dramatic effect on the fabric grain ... they often cause the crosswise threads—the weaker grain—to be pulled into a crooked or "off-grain" position. —"Fabric Finishes," page 69; "Grain and Fabric Finishes," page 93

I cannot speak Yiddish. Although I heard it every day growing up from my surrounding community and often from my mother, I never found the right voice or rhythm to use the language fluently in conversation. I suppose some of it rubbed off on me, though, as I can understand quite a bit of the sarcasm, wit, and expressiveness of this hybrid tongue, comprising high German, Slavic, Hebrew, and probably a splash of many other languages all rolled into one.

My mother was clear in her intention to cultivate a truly American daughter. Yiddish was not her first language since Hungarian Jews apparently spoke primarily Hungarian as their mother tongue in an attempt to assimilate into the larger culture. Yet she knew just enough Yiddish to join in easily among the greenhorn community. Many of them spoke it effortlessly. In our home, she spoke Yiddish at times, but discouraged my response in kind. English was the language I had to learn with the highest level of fluency.

A typical Yiddish/English dialogue during my adolescence may have sounded like this, on one of our frequent walks to Triangle Pharmacy, the family drugstore near the corner of Maryland and Dickinson Streets in the Forest Park neighborhood:

"Hanele, loyf nisht! Farvos azoy shnel? [Don't run! Why are you going so fast?]"

"Ma, I'm not running, just walking fast, that's all."

"Oy, Gottenu [Oh, dear Lord!]", she voiced in exasperation, using that ever-ubiquitous diphthong, "oy."

"I'll walk slower, okay?"

"*Take* [pronounced "tah-keh"]. *Du bist azoy voyle tokhter,*" she responded with sarcasm. Of course, you're such a nice daughter.

My mother died on Mother's Day 2006 at around 9:30 a.m. in her room at the nursing home. I knew within minutes of her soul leaving her physical body that I would eulogize her and include a segment of my eulogy in Yiddish at her funeral. An impulse had overwhelmed my subconscious so strongly that an internal voice spoke to me with surety that somehow, ensconced among my English words, I would express my true sentiments for her in Yiddish. I could not describe my emotions in any more meaningful way.

As I gave in to my instincts, I also knew that I would have to practice my Yiddish words carefully to ensure that I would pronounce them correctly, so that they would have a profound impact on those who heard them. Now, looking back, I wonder at my sheer boldness in voicing the first full sentences I had ever spoken in Yiddish at, of all places, my mother's funeral. Moreover, I would give my speech before a gathering of mourners that was sure to contain numerous Yiddish speakers. I would have to practice my words during the day and hope they took root in my sleep in order to be prepared on Tuesday morning, only two days later.

At Sidonia's gravesite

After my daughter, Brenda, spoke eloquently about her grandmother, I arose and expressed these words:

> "Zi hot geven mayn muter, mayn foter, mayn shvester, un mayn bruder, ale in eyn mentsh. Zi hot genehen azoy sheyner zakhn fur di gantse velt tsu zen. Ikh hob ir zeyer gelibt. [She was my mother, my father, my sister, and my brother, all in one person. She had sewn such beautiful things for the entire world to see. I loved her very much.]"

My Yiddish words expressed what had given my mother's life meaning: the fulfillment of a creative vision that contributed extraordinary beauty and style to the earth. She had lived a creatively fulfilling existence, if not one of personal happiness. Her life was not marked by a poignant love story that emerged from the embers of the Holocaust, nor a variety of eclectic accomplishments, nor significant wealth. Yet, she left this world as a "mentsh," bequeathing only the memory of her golden hands, exceptional imagination, and unflinching determination.

At the cemetery, a mixture of old and new friends joined my children in standing behind me as I watched her simple pine casket lowered into the earth. I barely noticed as a cool rain fell on our small party on that spring day in 2006. Tightly pursing my lips, caught up in a reverie of memories of my irascible mother, I could not cry. She was the strength, the centerpiece, upon which our partnership was based. Now, with the support of the new family I helped to create, I would have to find my way without her.

When the imaginary Sidonia was ninety, she began to display odd behavior, like forgetting how to start her car, the recipes to her favorite Hungarian dishes, or her grandchildren's names. David was concerned that his mother, who had lived alone since his father's death, may have dementia. After a physician's evaluation, his fears were confirmed. Sidonia was diagnosed with Alzheimer's disease, just as his father had been before her.

Although she wished to remain in her condominium on her own, David insisted that his mother come and live with him and his wife. Their children had grown and left home, leaving room for Sidonia to join them. Sarah was then working only part time and would take on caretaking duties. Reluctantly, Sidonia acceded to selling her condo and many of the furnishings and items she had held for many years, and moving in with David and Sarah.

Sidonia's stay with her son and daughter-in-law lasted only five months. She experienced restless nights marked by nightmares and hallucinations, reducing her sleep and causing dysfunction during her daytime hours. Like the real Sidonia, she suffered from the arthritis that had plagued her during much of her life and began to flare into sharp pain in her knees, making walking increasingly difficult. She needed more care than David and Sarah could provide. David was forced to arrange for her admission to the Jewish Nursing Home.

Sidonia found many of her contemporaries at the nursing home and joined in daily activities with them, such as bingo, music programs, and religious activities. Until her dementia progressed to the point of preventing participation, she enjoyed hearing about current events, as well. David and Sarah and her grandchildren, Vincent and Herman, came to visit her as often as their schedules would allow. During their visits, they were always surprised to see that many residents of the nursing home had no visitors, so they mingled with as many other residents as possible.

After two years in the nursing home, Sidonia's arthritis made walking impossible and, with great reluctance, she was transferred from a walker to a wheelchair. By the third year of her time there, she began to garble her speech and had lost much of her appetite, leading to severe weight loss.

This Sidonia never reverted back to the instincts that had saved her during the Holocaust. Even though she could no longer eat much of the food served at the nursing home, she did not feel the need to hoard leftovers. Her marriage with Henry had provided her with a safe and nurturing environment for so many years that it was that memory that remained with her when she was alone near the end of her life at the nursing home. She did not harken back to the days when food was a scarce commodity and starvation was rampant.

Sidonia died on Mother's Day in 2006 while David was at her side. Her life had contained many struggles, such as losing her entire family as a young woman, the horrors of the Holocaust, a misguided love affair, coming to a new country on her own, and later losing a son to drug abuse. Yet, it had also included a blissful marriage, ownership of a successful business and a lovely home, a brilliant and caring son, admiration from others for her cooking and sewing prowess, and a general feeling of contentment. My imagined Sidonia's life had been fulfilling, after all.

CHAPTER 32

Gathers

> Gathers are formed by drawing up fabric on a line of stitching. They are part of the design of a garment, supplying a soft fullness when needed ... stitching can be done with hand running stitch ... but is faster and more even when done by machine. When pressing, avoid flattening gathers, work point of iron into them.
> — "Gathers and Shirring," page 91

Only a few months after my mother's death, I decided to organize a reunion to gather together the children with whom I had grown up in Springfield. The memory of that early life helped to comfort me as I coped with losing my mother, and I felt a need to see my peers from the North End again, all of them offspring of Holocaust survivors. It was this group that knew me best, and more importantly, knew my mother. In the wake of losing my only family, I instinctively needed to see those who had surrounded my mother and me during our early years in America.

Thirteen of them joined me that fall at a large beach house that we rented over a long weekend so we could all be together. We had lived in close quarters as children so this seemed natural.

As I met some of them at the nearby train station or airport, or greeted them as they arrived after driving down to the beach, I recognized all of their faces, even though I had not seen many of them for almost forty years. They were all in their fifties and sixties then, older than the age at which I remembered most of their parents, the Holocaust survivors whom I knew so well in my youth. We embraced each other as though we were back in time on Osgood Street.

We ate our meals together over a three-day period, enjoyed strolls along the shore, and sat out lazily in Adirondack chairs facing the cove. Each of us had stories and memories of the characters that populated our childhood community and we told them with equal parts colorful humor and pathos. As we all gathered around the one television to play Scene It, a video game that tests players' knowledge of movie scenes, actors, titles, and obscure movie facts, the competition was keen and feisty. As predicted, Irma, the smartest one of us kids, a National Merit finalist in high school, had the most correct answers, but I think I might have been a worthy second best.

When the long weekend came to an end, I knew that I had done the right thing in gathering this group together to rekindle our long-ago friendships. In part, it was a selfish act that I hoped would comfort me in the wake of my mother's death. In that regard, it was successful. However, at the end of our getaway, I realized that it had heartened everyone else who attended, as well. Whatever trials and life conditions we had endured in the intervening years since we had lived together as children, seeing these friends, who had all lived with survivors of one of the most heinous events that had ever occurred, was good for the soul.

I often remember our shoreline gathering of childhood friends soon after my mother's death. At the time, the majority of our group of survivors' offspring was in relatively good health. Although one of our members reminded us then, "Now, we are the older generation. It's not our parents anymore," we still promised to bear witness to what our parents had endured far into the future. We felt invincible, as though old age and chronic disease would never hinder our daunting task of keeping our parents' stories, and our own experiences as their children, alive. We vowed to share them with the world, lest they suffer what Thomas Hardy described as "the second death … those whose story no one knows."

As the years have elapsed, a number of those who gathered have also gone to their death, taken by chronic disease, even the one who warned us that we had become the older generation instead of our parents. They are no longer able to carry on the story of loss, bravery, and resilience. Henceforth, the burden falls on those of us who remain to carry on the urgent deed.

CHAPTER 33

Tape Measure and Style

> Try not to stint on the quality of your equipment. Invest in the best and give it your best care. You don't need to buy it all at once … Tape measure [is] usually 60" long, with metal ends. A good tape measure will not stretch, and has measurements clearly marked on both sides. — "Equipment," page 64

> Remember that correct choice of figure type and size not only makes for good fit, but keeps alterations to a minimum … Select a style similar to one you have worn before and know is right for you … steer clear of complicated designs! — "Patterns," page 128

As I reflect on my upbringing, I am sometimes struck by the characteristics and behaviors that I have adopted through the years. I suppose I should not be so surprised. I can clearly see now that, in many cases, my habits and behavioral styles stem in a very direct way from the person and environment that helped to shape me the most. Here are my current measurements:

I am a woman with few notable talents or skills. This may seem too self-deprecating, but it really is not. For example, I am not a natural cook, but since I have to eat and occasionally entertain, I can muster simple meals, using numerous recipes for support. This is how I fed my family in my younger years.

I am not very artistic and have no skill in painting, sculpture, pottery, or graphic design. As mentioned, I cannot sew, not even a button or a straight seam. Actually, all needlework and crafts, for the most part, are too precise for my non-dexterous hands, now further limited by a bit of arthritic neuralgia. Nor do I possess any other significant domestic skills related to housekeeping or home organization and decor. Spatial relationships are beyond me.

I am a bit self-centered but reasonably intelligent. I am not very scientific or mathematical. Although I am fairly well read, I am not particularly conversant with classic or modern fiction. I lean more toward nonfiction, including history and biography. The American presidency and the holders of that office have always fascinated me. Even then, I often start and stop reading books. Sometimes I am reading several books at the same time, but not concentrating totally on any of them, often just extracting bits of trivia I find interesting.

I cannot remember nor can I tell a joke if my life depended on it. I do not sing well nor can I play an instrument, with the exception of easy ukulele songs. I appreciate music and can dance fairly well, as long as the steps are simple. Playing sports has never been my forte. If my TV, computer, cellphone, or any electronic device ceases to function, I would be lost, since I have no mechanical or technological skills to solve the problem. I could go on to list many other common human talents that have eluded me.

If I measure the breadth of assets I possess, I can identify a few characteristics that have probably allowed me to go through life mostly alone and without undue hardship. The first is my love for and proficiency with words. I like to pronounce them, roll them around my tongue and use them in sentences, preferably in the English language, but sometimes in other languages, as well, although much less fluently. My fondness for words enables me to express myself in a manner that is succinct, clear, and understandable, not superfluous nor esoteric. Knowledge of words has, undoubtedly, come in handy in my administrative and supervisory roles, as well as my literary ventures.

I also have a certain ability at trivia, which has waned somewhat as I age, but remains proficient, although I lack the fast response times needed for a game of Jeopardy. Some of my trivia knowledge may be useless for all intents and purpose, but some may have shed light on a time in history, an important person or event, or a significant invention that has changed the world. Whether my trivia wisdom has been useful or not, I cannot shut off the treasure trove of information crammed into my brain. It could have been my mother's insistence on acquiring knowledge that triggered my brain to record random bits of data.

No doubt my years of observing my mother have taught me the skill to proficiently manage my financial affairs. Like her, I probably have not invested my money wisely enough to earn significant financial gain. However, my past business decisions have put me in a contented economic state and I easily lead an independent life, free from economic worries. I am willing to avoid an extravagant lifestyle that might stretch my resources beyond their limits.

I have a deeply strong work ethic. My drive to complete an assignment can be so intense that it is often difficult to veer away from the task at hand. I experience great pleasure when my work achieves positive outcomes, particularly when it pertains to people I may have helped or mentored or to readers who have resonated with my written words. Despite the many years I worked for government, I have never been involved in governmental corruption or deception. My work has always helped to define me and I need to feel good about my reputation and myself. Even now, when many of my contemporaries have retired, I retain my ambition and quest for fresh vistas; I seem to be always occupied with a new project and working to give back to my community. I hope I can continue some of the work I love until I am at least ninety, like my mother.

Lastly, I know how to wear clothing. Even as I grow older, I can still show off skirts and dresses of varying lengths, a blazer jacket, a jersey or cotton top, skinny or wide-leg pants, a business suit, a fitted jacket, loose cover-up, or coat. Although these days my wardrobe is store-bought, it does not deviate very much from the styles I modeled when my mother was the sole creator of my attire. My outfits often tend to be chic, slim, sleek, and trendy, with little excess fabric or flourishes, such as ruffles or sewn or ironed-on decoration. The fit, shape, and fabric allow each clothing item to speak for itself. As usual, I wear my clothes with a straight back and my head and chin pointing up.

In the years since my mother's death, I have thought of her daily. She did not leave me many tangible items to call up her memory. A few twenty-dollar bills in bank envelopes in her safe deposit box and some old furnishings made up most of her non-sewing inheritance.

Aptly, it was her creative legacy that gave me the most consolation. Her Pfaff sewing machine now stands in its own alcove in my living room, looking almost the same as it did when my mother was toiling in front of it, intently moving a piece of cloth under its needle and presser foot. With no dressmaker using it, the machine's head has been inverted inside the wooden console to leave a flat surface on top for family photographs. Its drawers, still untouched, are filled with the items she stored inside: her pinking shears, hooks and eyes, snaps, thread spools, seam binding, and a plethora of bobbins, still wound with the threads of numerous sewing assignments.

The results of my mother's last thirty years at the sewing machine, including many of the garments and ensembles she designed and sewed for Brenda and me, remained in a closet until they caught the eye of a design connoisseur. These one-of-a-kind garments have since been collected in an exhibition that travels to various venues, where visitors can view my mother's genius first-hand.

Sidonia's Seam Binding 241

Opening night of "Sidonia's Thread Exhibition," 2019. With curator, Anya Sokolovskaya, Associate Professor of Costume Design, Eastern Connecticut State University. At the Windham Textile and History Museum, Windham, Conn.

Realizing that she, in large part, shaped whatever skills I do possess, I wish my mother could have been with me to share in the joyful events that have occurred since she left this earth. She would have been proud to attend the wedding of her grandson, Stephen, to his bride, Elena, only four years after she was gone. She would surely have fallen in love with her great grandchildren, Brenda and Michael's children, Lauren and Sydney, and Stephen and Elena's children, Kate and Chloe. Each of these descendants carries the legacy of their grandmother and great-grandmother, who had the strength of character and powerful will to build a noble life despite her shattering losses.

The author's grandchildren, Lauren, Chloe, Kate, and Sydney

CHAPTER 34

Thread and Needle

> Thread and needle, without which no sewing could be done, are practically a unit. Not only is one useless without the other, but, to do a proper job, they must be suited to each other. And, above all, to the fabric you want them to stitch ... Choose your thread according to your fabric—heavier thread for heavier fabric, lighter thread for lighter fabric. —"Thread and Needles," page 164

My wandering imagining of an alternate reality of my mother's life has led me to two conclusions. According to my view, had I not been born, there was a good chance that my mother, Sidonia, would have experienced a more fulfilling romantic partnership and would have had children who evoked, on one hand, immense gratification, but unfortunately, on the other hand, considerable regret and helplessness. My alternative reality could not spare her the sadness and disappointment of losing a child she loved. Still, at the same time, she might have met the love of her life and lived as a *baleboste*, the accomplished housewife of her dreams, a goal that in real life eluded her. I so wish she could have lived that reality.

However, in this imagined reality, it was also possible that her significant design talent would not have had the opportunity to fully emerge and the world might never have known her exemplary skill. No one would have acted as the partner she needed to display her bountiful creative gift, no one to accede to her wishes time after time, and no one willing to listen, without interruption, to her tales of happiness and misery.

Other alternative realties, of course, were possible, but the only one my imagination could evoke was the one to which I consistently returned. I could not envision any other.

As I finally wrap up the story of two women who faced the world together with strength and determination, I am convinced that the reason I was born was ultimately to provide redemption for my mother. That must have been why, despite all the challenges in our life together, we still seemed to fit like needle and thread.

Although, surely, to borrow the words I have read in my *Lev Shalem* prayer book during the High Holy Days, I have been unworthy, yet I am brought "joyfully to the fullness of redemption." Amid her troubling emotions of loss, shame, and regret, my mother attained a fulfillment of her deep creative desires, which was long nurtured throughout her life in America. If I was the catalyst that allowed it to occur, I am proud and satisfied. Aside from raising my children, it easily supersedes any other accomplishment I may have achieved in my life.

These days, when I get up each morning and look into the bathroom mirror, I see my mother's face. So many years after her death, I observe her high cheekbones and her pointed chin on my increasingly aged face as though they are embedded in mine. My mixed hazel and green eyes remind me of hers in the haunted photograph she used for her visa document to enter the United States. Age seems to have enhanced my facial resemblance to my mother. In my youth, our faces looked nothing alike, except perhaps for our high cheekbones. No one would have noted any other similarities in our features. Yet, lately, when I encounter those who knew her, quite a few remark upon our similar visages, and tell me I evoke such vivid memories of her.

When I am ready to dress, I gaze at the voluminous wardrobe choices that face me in my closet and I often unconsciously select outfits I know would have gained her approval. Shunning nightgowns or pajamas during the day, unless I am too ill to rise from bed, I always dress as though I am headed to an in-person business meeting, outing, or other human interaction, even if I am staying home. With my stable weight—a remnant of my mother's stringent training—my clothing remains well fitted.

As I age, I recognize that I also take on more of her behavior patterns, like her solitary nature, her stubbornness, and her headstrong pride and ambition. I no longer resist resembling my mother's visage or her personality, or even revealing some of her secrets. Moreover, except for a few deviations, the course of my life hewed very close to her vision.

This is me. I am Sidonia's daughter.

Acknowledgments

Writing this last volume in the *Sidonia's Thread* trilogy was equally as emotional as writing its two predecessors, *Sidonia's Thread* and *Surviving Remnant*. Just as with the first two, this book has caused me to comb the strands of my memory and its associated events and emotions, and most importantly, explore the best means to express and convey them to the reader. I have required five years between each book to navigate my memory and choose just the right words. To add to the mix, this book also includes an alternative reality interspersed with real-life events—a daunting and difficult task—and a return to the use of sewing methods as chapter titles, paralleling the events described therein.

I have called upon a number of friends, family, and advisors to help me sort through the maze of all that I wish to express in this book. As usual, my children, Brenda Marcus Bula and Stephen Marcus, have given me their insights, from their own personal perspectives, regarding the dynamics of my relationship with my mother, Sidonia, a perspective that they alone possess. Brenda also read the manuscript at various stages of development and offered her sage advice. Their humor and clarity succeeded in lightening the emotional load of turning my recollections and imagination into a series of memoirs.

My friends from my social work days for both the Town of Manchester and City of Hartford, Connecticut, continue to be a source of support and strength in my writing career. Even though I have not provided social work services for almost two decades, their friendship remains as steadfast as ever. Many thanks to Eleanor Beaulieu, Sue Bernstein, Jo Miller, Beth Mix, Nancy Simonds, Beth Stafford, Deborah Stein, and Diane Wicks for their ongoing encouragement.

Two of my Manchester friends assisted me in reading my manuscript at different stages. Nancy Simonds read the volume in its infancy and gave me her honest guidance about my next steps, and also proofread it in the very final stages. Deborah Stein acted as one of my official manuscript readers after the first round of editing and offered her wisdom.

Diane DeFronzo, one of my earliest friends and colleagues from my time in Hartford, agreed to review the manuscript, as well. Her thorough and specific suggestions for improvements, accomplished in person at my kitchen counter, truly changed the manuscript for the better.

Three fellow authors and respected advisors acted as manuscript readers. Steve Leshin, author of the Joshua Oates adventure series, offered advice regarding structure and format; Penny Goetjen, the famed mystery writer, who resonated with some of the themes of my book, offered input on clarity and story flow; and Barbara Bergren, author of *Witness for My Father*, provided encouragement and guidance on word usage (sometimes less is more), and inspired a revisit to the story's alternative reality.

My editor, Sarah Gilligan, spent a concentrated period of time with me, frequently through virtual meetings, advising me on aspects of the story, including word usage, content and flow, grammar, and structure. Her professional guidance was invaluable.

Mary Crombie, of Acorn Studio, provided the graphic design for the interior and exterior of the book. As I also entrusted her with the design of my previous book, *Surviving Remnant*, I owe her a debt of gratitude again for making this new volume look so enticing.

Finally, I would like to thank the marketing team at Coats

& Clark, Inc., now a division of SPINRITE, for their permission to reprint material from, *Coats & Clark's Sewing Book: Newest Methods from A to Z*, which introduces each chapter title and opening epigraph. Sidonia was a devoted user of Coats & Clark thread. Excerpts from their book are a fitting tribute to her masterful stitchery.

Bibliography

Adlington, Lucy. *The Dressmakers of Auschwitz: The True Story of the Women Who Sewed to Survive*. New York: HarperCollins, 2021.

Bart, Michael and Lauren Corona. *Until Our Last Breath: A Holocaust Story of Love and Partisan Resistance*. New York: St. Martin's Press, 2008.

Bergren, Barbara. *Witness for My Father: A World War II Story of Loss, Hope, and Discovery*. Middletown: Sandkey Press, 2020.

Bierman, John. *Righteous Gentile: The Story of Raoul Wallenberg, Missing Hero of the Holocaust*. New York: The Viking Press, 1981.

Coats & Clark Educational Bureau. *Coats & Clark's Sewing Book: Newest Methods from A to Z*. New York: Educational Bureau of Coats & Clark, Inc., 1967.

"Dachau Concentration Camp: History and Overview (March 8, 1933–April 29, 1945)." *Jewish Virtual Library*. https://www.jewishvirtuallibrary.org/history-and-overview-of-dachau.

Dámóc, Hungary. *City-Facts*. http://www.city-facts.com/damoc/population. Accessed March 28, 2023.

Deiler, Manfred. "Women in the Kaufering/Landsberg Concentration Camp: Gisela Stone's Story of Survival." Translated by Sally LeBold. *Landsberger Zeitgeschichte*. European Holocaust Memorial Foundation, 2016. https://landsberger-zeitgeschichte.de/Geschichte/geschichte/stoneentgl.htm.

Donn, Rabbi Hayim Halevy. *To Be a Jew: A Guide to Jewish Observance in Contemporary Life*. New York: Basic Books, 1972.

Field, Rabbi Edward, Rabbi Leonard Gordon, Rabbi Stuart Kelman, Rabbi Alan Lettofsky, Cantor Joseph Levine, Cantor Ken Richmond, Rabbi Robert Scheinberg, Rabbi Laurence Sebert, Rabbi Jan Robyn Urbach, Rabbi Jan Caryl Kaufman. *Mahzor Lev Shalem for Rosh Hashanah and Yom Kippur*. Edited by Rabbi Edward Field. New York: The Rabbinical Assembly, Inc., 2010.

Frankl, Viktor E. *Man's Search for Meaning*. Part One translated by Ilse Lasch. Boston: Beacon Press, 1959, 1962, 1984, 1992, 2006.

Galvin, Herman and Stan Tamarkin. *The Yiddish Dictionary Sourcebook: A Transliterated Guide to the Yiddish Language*. Hoboken: Ktav Publishing House, Inc., 1986.

Hardy, Thomas. "The To-be-forgotten." *RPO (Representative Poetry Online)*. RPO edition 1998. https://rpo.library.utoronto.ca/content/be-forgotten.

Harrington, Michael. *The Other America: Poverty in the United States*. Baltimore: Penguin Books, 1963.

Holland, Kimberly. "What is Transference?" Medically reviewed by Timothy J. Legg, PhD., PsyD. *Healthline*. May 28, 2019. https://www.healthline.com/health/mental-health/transference.

"Hungarian, Flour Bag Seal, Louisen Steam Mill." March 25, 2018. *Gallery.* https://bagseals.org/_001_001/jrmcleodDampfmuhlFlourBagSeal.

"JewishGen Unified Search: The JewishGen Hungary Database." *JewishGen.* https://jewishgen.org/databases/jgform.php.

Johnson, Dirk. "Yale's Limit on Jewish Enrollment Lasted Until Early 1960s, Book Says." the *New York Times,* March 6, 1986. https://www.nytimes.com/1986/03/04/nyregion/yale-s-limit-on-jewish-enrollment-lasted-until-early-1960-s-book-says.html.

Karsa, Elek. "Facts and Data on the History of the Ghetto in Ujhely." Chapter X. 135-149. *Vanished Communities in Hungary.* Found in *JewishGen.* https://jewishgen.org/yizkor/Satoraljaujhely/sate134.html.

Levi, Primo. *Survival in Auschwitz: The Nazi Assault on Humanity.* Translated by Stuart Woolf. New York: First Collier Books, 1993.

Marcus, Hanna Perlstein. *Sidonia's Thread: The Secrets of a Mother and Daughter Sewing a New Life in America.* New Charleston: CreateSpace, 2012.

———. *Surviving Remnant: Memories of the Jewish Greenhorns in 1950s America.* Middletown: Buttonhole Publishing, 2017.

Margaritoff, Marco. "44 Tragic Photos Taken Inside the Nazi's Bergen Belsen Concentration Camp." Checked by Leah Silverman, June 9, 2019. Updated July 28, 2019. *All That's Interesting.* https://allthatsinteresting.com/bergen-belsen.

Mendelsohn, Daniel. *The Lost: A Search for Six of Six Million.* New York: HarperCollins, 2006.

Neil, Cecily and Markku Tykkylainen. *Local Economic Development: A Geogratorphical Comparison of Rural Community Restructuring.* New York: United Nations University Press, 1998.

Postrel, Virginia. *The Fabric of Civilization: How Textiles Made the World.* New York: Basic Books, 2020.

Proverbs 31:28, JPS Tanakh 1917. *Bible Hub.* https://biblehub.com/jps/proverbs/31.htm. Accessed March 27, 2023

Reihman, Lynn. "Beginning Where the Client Is: Social Casework Intervention in Direct Work with Families Who Are Poor." In *Poverty and Social Casework Services: Selected Papers.* Edited by Ben A. Orcutt. Metuchen: The Scarecrow Press, Inc., 1974.

Roth, Philip. *Goodbye, Columbus* in *Philip Roth: Novels and Stories (1959–1962).* The Library of America, 2005.

Rothbart, Jacob M. "Jewish Craftsmen and Occupations in Gombin." 13–23. *JewishGen.* https://jewishgen.org/yizkor/gombin/gom028.html.

Sas, Meir. "From Equity to Holocaust." Chapter IX. 110-133. *Vanished Communities in Hungary: The History and Tragic Fate of the Jews in Ujhely and Zemplen County.* Found in *JewishGen.* https://jewishgen.org/yizkor/Satoraljaujhely/sate110.html.

———. "Jewish Communities in Zemplén." *Vanished Communities in Hungary: The History and Tragic Fate of the Jews in Ujhely and Zemplen County*, Chapter XI. 150–162. *JewishGen.* https://jewishgen.org/yizkor/Satoraljaujhely/sate134.html.

Seltzer, Leon S. "Subconscious vs. Unconscious: How to Tell the Difference." *Psychology Today*. Posted December 4, 2019. https://www.psychologytoday.com/us/blog/evolution-the-self/201912/subconscious-vs-unconscious-how-tell-the-difference.

Siska, József. *Dámóc: Története És Népe [History and People]*. Edited by Dr. Daniel Kováts. Sátoraljaújhely City Council: Ferenc Daragó, Publisher, 1987.

United States Holocaust Memorial Museum, Washington, DC. "Auschwitz." *Holocaust Encyclopedia*. Last edited March 16, 2015. https://encyclopedia.ushmm.org/content/en/article/auschwitz.

———. "Bergen-Belsen." *Holocaust Encyclopedia*. Last edited April 13, 2020. https://encyclopedia.ushmm.org/content/en/article/bergen-belsen.

———. "Bergen Belsen Displaced Persons Camp." *Holocaust Encyclopedia*. Accessed October 2022. https://encyclopedia.ushmm.org/content/article/bergen-belsen-displaced-persons-camp.

———. "Bergen Belsen in Depth: The Camp Complex." *Holocaust Encyclopedia*. Accessed November 2022. https://encyclopedia.ushmm.org/content/en/article/bergen-belsen-in-depth-the-camp-complex.

University of Massachusetts, Amherst. "150 Years of UMASS Amherst History." 2013. https://umass.edu/150/timeline.

Wasserman, Henry. "Tailoring." *Encyclopaedia Judaica*. Gale Group, 2008. Found in Jewish Virtual Library. https://jewishvirtuallibrary.org/tailoring.

———. "Textiles (Sections on Central Europe and Hungary)." *Encyclopaedia Judaica*. Gale Group, 2008. Found in Jewish Virtual Library. https://jewishvirtuallibrary.org/textiles.

Weiner, Myron E. *Human Services Management: Analysis and Applications*. Belmont: Wadsworth Publishing Company, 1990.

Weintraub, Rabbi Simkha Y. "Jewish Prayer for the Sick, Mi Sheberach." *My Jewish Learning*. https://myjewishlearning.com/article/mi-sheberakh-may-the-one-who-blessed/.

Wex, Michael. *Born to Kvetch: Yiddish Language and Culture in All of Its Moods*. New York: HarperCollins, 2006.

Wiesel, Elie. *Night*. New York: Hill and Wang, 2006.

Wilson, Jennifer. "Creating Beauty in the Wake of the Holocaust: Jewish Holocaust Survivors and Their Post-War Careers in the Clothing Industry." MHGS Thesis, Gratz College, 2019.

———. Educators' Guide for "Sidonia's Thread: Crafting a Life from Holocaust to High Fashion" exhibition. Eastern Connecticut State University, 2021. https://sidoniasthreadexhibit.org.

Illustration Credits

All photographs and documents are from the author's or her family's collection unless otherwise noted.

Chapter 1, Figure 1: This early photo of *di grine* is courtesy of the child at the farthest right, Miriam Citron Burhans.

Chapter 6, Figure 1: Photo by Dan Roggi for the "Sidonia's Thread Exhibition," originally in color. All photos by Dan Roggi were for the "Sidonia's Thread Exhibition" and were originally in color.

Chapter 10, Figure 2: "Best Dressed Coed" is taken from the author's copy of the University of Massachusetts student newspaper, *The Massachusetts Daily Collegian*, around 1966.

Chapter 11, Figure 1: Sidonia's Dachau Concentration Camp Questionnaire, *Konzentrationslager Dachau,* Prisoner Number 86794, Perstein [sic] Szidonia, is from the United States Holocaust Memorial Museum, International Tracing Service collection, document number 10238447.

Chapter 16, Figure 2: The barleycorn tweed pants suit also has a matching skirt not shown. Photo by Dan Roggi.

Chapter 18, Figure 1: Sidonia's birth certificate originated from the county registry office for Borsod-Abaúj-Zemplén county, located in Miskolc, Hungary. Received in 1975.

Chapter 20, Figures 3–6: Photos by Dan Roggi.

Chapter 22, Figure 1: The ancestral photograph is courtesy of Bernat and Mari's great-granddaughter, Melanie Hall.

Chapter 25, Figures 3, 5, 6: Photos by Dan Roggi.

Chapter 29, Figure 3: The photo originally appeared in the *Springfield Republican.*

Chapter 30, Figure 1: Photo by Dan Roggi.

www.ingramcontent.com/pod-product-compliance
Lightning Source LLC
LaVergne TN
LVHW041612070426
835507LV00008B/200